Table of Contents

PREFACE

When man lost the divine provisions in the garden of Eden to disobedience, fear crept into his life and has been his torment since then. The devil has used the instrumentality of fear to keep man under his control; terrorize, incapacitate and blindfold him to God's redemptive provisions which is to restore man's loss. The heaven's resources will be of no value to man as long as he can be chained down by this ungodly fear.

This book sets out to remove the covering of the devil's deceit and manipulation through fear, and free children of God to enjoy all God has in stock for us. Free to display all divine potentials in us and enjoy divine benefits freely given to us.

One of great impairments brought to man through his fall is that he is rendered sensual and carnal, making his sense organs available for Satan to deliver his message of fear. A new transformation is brought to man through the new birth (salvation) that tunes his senses in line with God, by His Spirit, and word and awakens our spirits to God.

The new experience by His Spirit and word is to create a new form or brand of 'fear' in us; loving, trusting, reverence fear of God that holds His word as supreme and final authority on every issue of life and godliness.

This book, Dynamics of Fear, is sent as a divine instrument to the nations to bring healing and health to the body of Christ from the destruction caused by the devil's type of fear in Jesus Christ name.

Dr Akintunde Akintayo

INTRODUCTION

It is both timely and expedient for this work to be made available in this age and time for humanity. This is ironically a time when news of suicide has become a daily occurrence; divorce rate is high and low self-esteem is common amongst others in spite of the so many advancements in psychology, medical science and technology.

This book, when properly comprehended without bias will serve as a great tool for psychologists who are helping the teaming victims of psychological breakdown in today's world.

I urge the reader to follow with a keen mind and a heart that is willing to discover and adhere to the truth that can set free.

For Christians worldwide, this is a must read because like many others in the world, fear has always been Satan's subtle weapon that has kept us away from the main assignment we were called out to do. One of my heroes of the faith, Dr. David Livingstone, was able to live above fear and this empowered him to go where many will not, in a time and generation as his.

For years I could not take a bold step to start the work I was created and called to do due to fear. I questioned where will my next rent will come from? My next wears? My next meal? Unnecessary fears they all were. But glory be to God Almighty our heavenly father who patiently follows after us and does not give up on us.

Satan and his cohorts are subtly overpowering and destroying us through many forms of fear, it is time to talk about it and get out of it completely.

Get set to discover truths revealed by the Holy Spirit to set free from all fears and be free indeed. John 8:32.

As you read on, several prayer points are made available to help readers to connect in conversation with God concerning this matter and to also resist the enemy vehemently. Please do pause and pray these prayers before reading on. Pray like a combatant.

Hear this encouragement from the Lord John 16:33 (NIV)

"I have told you these things, so that in me you may have peace. In this world you will have trouble. But take heart! I have overcome the world."

SHALOM.

DYNAMICS OF FEAR
Pastor.OLUDADE Frank

e-mail: mawutoolufade@gmail.com
+2348035798630

ISBN- 978-978-54601-8-6
E-Book ISBN- 879-897-60451-3-0

Printed in Nigeria by Bi-Rit Publishing House
+2348164167804

ISBN (hardcover) 978-978-54601-8-6

Dedication

This book is dedicated to all who have been held back from being what they were created to be due to so much noise clouding their hearts and minds. It's time for manifestations.

Acknowledgments

My appreciation goes to my Father, God, Lord and Redeemer. In the person of Jesus Christ the only true potentate who is, was and is to come. The only wise God.

A big thank you to my parents Mr. and Mrs. J. O. Balogun for your tireless efforts and trainings over the years. Your lives are a great model for me. You have brought up great men. God bless you.

My gratitude also goes to my uncle and his wife daddy and mummy A. A. Ishola. Your positive contributions in my life can only be rewarded by God. Thank you.

Mummy Charity Igwe and mummy Janet Nuhu Anung, God bless you both greatly for the sacrifices made on me. My today is because the two of you played remarkable roles in my life.

I will also like to appreciate Dr. Akintunde Akintayo for all the words of mentorship over the years. The things I learnt from you sir have really come handy in my life.

My gratitude also goes to pastor Dele Oke of Dove Media. You've being a father and a mentor. Thank you for the trust given me over the years. God bless you sir.

I also appreciate all members of The Redeemed Christian Church of God, His Glory Area Headquarters parish, Shendam, Plateau state, Nigeria. Thank you all for believing in me as your pastor. God bless you all.

My siblings Felix, Frederick and Felicia. I appreciate you guys. My profound gratitude also to my cousins; Ronke, Adeola, Adejoke, Gbenga and Johnson, God bless you guys.

My profound gratitude to a friend and brother, pastor Jacob Pangtul Tali. Thank you for all the battles fought together, and all the lessons learnt from you. Those privileges God gave me with you are great teachers for me.

Also to my friends, colleagues and partners: pastor Basil Onyedimma, Rev. Sanni Francis, pastor Bisi Olawale and pastor Emmanuel Bukar. We have prayed together, learnt together, wrestled together and seen great results together. God bless you all.

To my very own sister Faith Donatus I say God bless you greatly in Jesus name. You have being a great encourager to me. Thank you.

Mr. Lomka Illiya Kopdiya, thank you for painstakingly taking time out of your busy schedule to edit this work. God bless you.

For sake of space I say thank you to all the people God gave me opportunity to meet over the years who have contributed in no little way in my life to make this a reality, God bless.

CHAPTER 1

FEAR AND ITS SOURCES

WHEN PEACE LIKE A RIVER

Verse1.

> When peace like a river
>
> Attendeth my way,
>
> When sorrows like seas billows roll;
>
> Whatever my lot, Thou has taught me to know,
>
> It is well, it is well with my soul.

Chorus.

> It is well, ... with my soul
>
> It is well, it is well with my soul.

Horatio Gates Spafford, a successful lawyer and businessman in Chicago married Anna and was blessed with five children. Their young son died of pneumonia in 1871, and in that same year, much of their business was lost to the great Chicago fire. Yet, God mercifully allowed the business to flourish again.

November 21, 1873 Mr. Spafford sent his wife and their four daughters to cross to Europe via the French ocean liner, Ville du Havre across the Atlantic, ahead of him due to some business problems he was to stay back in Chicago to resolve. He planned on joining them later.

Four days into crossing the Atlantic, the Ville du Harve collided with another larger ship and the Ville du Harve sank into the Atlantic carrying with it 226 of the 313 passengers on board including the four Spafford daughters.

Anna, floating, unconscious on a piece of the wreckage was spotted by a sailor rowing a small boat over the spot of the sinking and was rescued.

Nine days later, they landed in Cardiff, Wales, having being picked up by another larger vessel after the accident. From there she wired her husband a message which read: "Saved Alone, What Shall I Do?"

As he got the message, Mr. Spafford booked passage on the next available ship and left to join his grieving wife. Four days into the journey, the captain called Spafford to his cabin and told him they were over the place where his children went down.

According to Bertha Spafford Vester, a daughter born after the tragedy, Spafford wrote the prose: "IT IS WELL WITH MY SOUL" while on this journey.

The prose was later composed into a hymn by hymn composer Philip Paul Bliss.

(https://www.staugustine.com/living/religion/2014-10-16/story-behind-song-it-well-my-soul)

Those words were from a bereaved heart but certainly not from a fearful one. Those words came out of a life that lost very precious things, but not from a life that has lost faith or boldness in the God of salvation.

Fear works to make us ask the wrong questions and react wrongly. These, Horatio never gave in to.

Horatio Spafford may be long dead, yet not forgotten anytime this hymn is sung. That is what victory over fear does. Men still live long after they are gone when they overcome fear.

Someone said; "Peace is not the absence of trouble, but the state of calm and confidence in the midst of trouble."

"Fear", I say, "is that state of chaos, and dismay in spite of any condition or situation around"

When we say DYNAMICS, it is;

"the way in which people or things behave and react to each other in a particular situation."

While FEAR on the other hand is defined as;

"The bad feeling that you have when you are in danger, that something bad might happen, or when a particular thing frightens you."

Those who have experienced fear understand that feeling. It comes upon you, and the feeling goes on to make you behave in a particular way. What is really behind that feeling?

We will know later.

So, **"Dynamics of Fear is Actually The Way The Feelings That Fear Gives Makes You Behave, And React To The Corresponding Issues or Situations."**

Those feelings birth the workings of fear.

Example.

If all of a sudden the fear of being hit by a vehicle when crossing the road at a particular spot comes upon you while you walked along the road, the feeling certainly could make you behave or react in a particular way as regards that spot on the road; either you do not cross at all or you will change the spot, to cross the road from another side.

Fear is really powerful, or better put, deadly. The reason is that its feelings causes those under its influence to behave or react in particular manners. Little wonder Satan rules his kingdom using fear.

Take a study on fearful people and you will discover a resemblance of patterns in their ways of approach to things or situations.

Let us see the very first response to fear in humanity. It happened to the man called Adam and his wife, Eve.

Genesis 3:8 – 12

Let us see the pattern of behavior and the reactions of Adam when fear brought that feeling on him.

1. He fled - ran away - from seeing God.

2. He hid himself among some things.

3. He kept himself where God - no one - will see him.

I Samuel 10:21 – 23

I Kings 19:2 - 4

From this scriptures, you will notice familiar patterns in the behavior of those under the influence of fear.

Fleeing.

Hiding among things

Keeping ourself from being seen. (Running away

From possible solutions and helps)

Throughout the bible, when you check several scriptures, similar patterns are repeated. A good example is found in I Samuel 13:6

Whenever the thought of hiding away by reason of this negative feelings comes to anyone, know certainly that fear is at work.

This response of hiding away is the reason why a husband closes from work and refuses to go home until he is certain that his wife is asleep. Why?

There is a feeling of fear he gets by the presence of his wife. This can be vice-versa, including children and parents.

It is the same feeling that makes a man scared of coming in contact with old successful acquaintances etc. Some prefer to hide away since they feel they are not good enough in their own eyes as compared to the achievements of others.

Fear is so dangerous because of what it does to those under its influence.

It motivates one to do things that are wrong just to please others.

"Hides" one from trying again.

"Hides" one from asking for forgiveness.

"Hides" one from admitting wrong or error, or sin.

"Hides" from starting that idea or vision.

"Hides" from telling your own side of the story.

"Hides" from standing out and to publicly declare your faith in Jesus Christ.

"Hides" from breaking away from that system or habit.

Worst of all, it "hides" one among ideologies, philosophies and wisdoms that your heart or conscience tells you cannot be true.

Such could be responsible for the belief in what we find today as the evolutionary theory which is totally senseless.

Fear is quite dangerous.

One danger of fear is that it transcends the time or season or age of those it grabs with its influence.

The human race got to this point because Adam and Eve, Adam especially, was afraid to admit his wrong, and afraid to come out to meet God who came in search of him. Humanity has not stopped being afraid since then.

Thank God for people like Winston Churchill, Martin Luther the reformer and Martin Luther King Junior who trampled fear underfoot. These men, in their days charged against fear to stop it from its sources – Nazi tyranny, the clutches of heresies that ruled the church, and racism. You and I must not tremble before fear, but be reminded that; "God has not given us a spirit of fear, but of power, of love and of sound mind."

We must hate fear with perfect hatred. Every satanic terrifying and limiting fear must be quenched completely.

I would love to leave this important point with you;

As bad as fear is, you must know that fear has two sides or sources:

SOURCES OF FEAR

1. The first source of fear is God. This is what is called the fear of God.

Examples:

Genesis 20:11, 22:12, 42:18

Exodus 1:17, Job 28:28

Proverbs 3:7 says;

"Do not be wise in your own eyes; fear the Lord and shun evil."

This is the only kind of fear that is valuable to all humans on the planet; the fear of God. We will treat it in details later in chapter 7.

Please take note of this very important point, God allows this fear in man for a good purpose. That we all may look out for one another and seek each other's good.

Isaiah 59:19, 57:11

Satan, as usual is a corrupter. By manipulations and lies he corrupts this positive fear to use it for his own benefit. This brings us to the second source of fear.

2. This second source is of the devil. This is the fear that stops a man from carrying out good things to better his life and those of others around him. This is the fear that cripples a man making him a nonentity.

A perfect example of one who overcame this kind of fear is Nick Vujicic, the Australian Christian Evangelist. Though without limbs, his life is a greater success story than many with limbs. Why?

Nick does not have room for Satan's fear, and so he is not crippled or limbless within.

PLEASE TAKE NOTE:

There Cannot Be Two Lords Controlling A Particular Life. Just as No Two Drivers Can Both Be on the Driver's Seat at The Same Time in a Car.

Refusal of One Source of Fear Means Acceptance of the Other Source.

HOW THEN DOES FEAR BEGIN?

Let us take some case studies to analyze this.

1.

Genesis 3:6-10

He and his wife had just done something and that action gave them a knowing, but it was not the right knowing they should have had.

a.   Genesis 3:7

A New Sense

Their eyes were opened.

This means they began to analyze things from a different angle or perspective than how they used to in the past.

This also meant they were now predisposed to a new sense. A sense that was not permitted to do anything before. Some people will tell you they just discovered that they are this or that and not what they actually are. That is fear at work. Example; "I just discovered I'm gay." Rubbish. That is fear my friend, deal with it.

b.   A Definition of Self

Verse 7 "..., and they knew that they were naked;..."

A new knowledge dawned on them. What was this knowledge?

They saw themselves in another light. They began to give a new definition to themselves contrary to what God gave them.

See this scenario;

Numbers 13:17-33

Ten out of the twelve spies had, or began to believe a new knowledge about themselves which they sold out to the people. In that knowledge, they gave a new definition of their nature and being. They said they were like grasshoppers.

Whenever you see a man beginning to give a new definition – negative – about himself, know for sure that fear has set in.

See this case also in Exodus 3:10 – 4:13

This same Moses who in Exodus 2:11-14 believed to be a prince and judge as well as a savior for Israel suddenly began to confess to God a new identity or definition. This definition came out of fear after forty years of what seemed like failure in the desert. His definitions include:

(Exodus 3:11) I am a no-body, "...who am I "

(Exodus 4:10) I am a stutterer; I stammer.

The same thing that fear did to Moses was what it did to Adam. It does same to anyone under its grip.

Adam and Eve gave in to the fear that kept them in that new state – or new self-realization – and it did them no good.

24

Hear this, many books and new age teachers talk of self-realization. This goes on to paint a totally different you to you, giving you new definitions about yourself that do you no good, but only cause you sorrow.

c.   **LIMITED BY LACK**

In defining themselves from a different angle, they gave concrete reasons why they were not fit for any good thing anymore.

"... I was afraid because I was naked;..." (Gen 3:10)

To be naked means ;

I do not have the right clothes for this.

I do not possess the right talents to be part of this.

I do not have the resources for this goal.

My age is against me, I am past the age.

I do not have the faith to receive this from God.

I am not eloquent enough for that.

Fear creeps in, silently reminding you of everything you lack, telling you not to make another attempt.

What Adam said could mean;

"I do not have what it takes to meet with you Lord"

When in actual sense, God had seen what he and Eve had done, and had decided to come to them, despite what they had or had not, to meet Him –God.

God saw that they really lacked some things, but that was inconsequential if only they had not lost the right definition of who they are, as God had told them. If only they had not redefined themselves in the name of self-realization.

d.   **SPIRITUAL NAKEDNESS**

Another way that fear creeps in is through a state of spiritual nakedness. How?

Genesis 3:7, 10

Let me ask a question,

If in this time or age of civilization, leaves were used for clothes or covering, would one then be correct to say I was naked if he/she had some leaves as covering?

Well, answer.

 A "No" will be the right answer I believe.

In verse 7, Adam and his wife sewed leaves together to cover their nakedness, yet in verse 10 he said unto God that he was naked.

That is a state of spiritual nakedness, confusion. A response that sounds something like:

"It's either this or that, well, I don't know, any will do." This sounds like what was going on in Adam's mind.

The same thought that goes on in a spiritually naked mind.

Spiritual nakedness in any mind proves the presence of fear in such a life.

This nakedness accounts for why they hid and would not come out. They hid among the trees. Just like the ten spies that went to spy out Canaan with Joshua and Caleb. These ten hid among the congregation to make sure they do not go for war.

Saul the son of Kish hid among the equipment in

I Samuel 10:21 – 23. Spiritual nakedness does this. It gives a sense of constant danger, so people keep hiding. Hiding in cultism or the occult, witchcraft, drugs etc.

Where Are You Hiding?

In the office?

On social media?

In the park?

In your father's house?

In excuses?

In addictions (Pornography, drugs etc)

Or video games?

2.

Now, above all these, fear really creeps in as it did in Adam and Eve's case when our eyes and attention is taken off God to some other things.

Adam and Eve took their eyes away from God and gave it to the serpent and their eyes began to see wrongly, their awareness began to change to a another one, they then defined themselves based on so called self-realization; this was what turned mankind into a confused entity who started hiding from things, in the midst of things. Out of fear.

Out fear of an afterlife, many have hidden in some things and have consistently given their eyes to those things in a false hope that those things will save them from the realities of afterlife. It is time to arise and ignore what anyone is saying that is contrary to the truth. Get your eyes off them and fix it where it should be. What you focus your eyes on determines your fears.

King Saul was one man that walked in fear right from the beginning and he never dealt with it until fear destroyed him. Fear destroyed King Saul and all his sons.

Fear does not just kill its host, if care is not taken, fear goes on to kill even descendants of the host.

Adam and Eve permitted it and humanity faces its dire consequences till today. Thank God for Jesus Christ.

In I Samuel 10:1, 9 – 11, we read of Saul's encounter with God, but then in I Samuel 10:20 -24, see the same Saul who had just encountered God in magnificent ways.

Saul hid because he did not see a king in himself; he saw in himself an ordinary farmer, and a lost donkey tracker. That is all that his life amounts to in his own sight.

Saul quickly took his eyes away from God and was almost replaced from the very moment he was selected for coronation, had God not mercifully intervened. Yet he continued in the fear that later took his eyes off God; when in I Samuel 13:8 – 12, out of fear he offered up burnt offerings that he was not authorized to.

Also in I Samuel 15:24, Saul, out of fear obeyed the people and ignored God. That was the final straw that broke the camel's back for king Saul. God had had enough of his fears and the fact that he was not doing anything about it.

Fear kept crippling Saul by sowing pride, bitterness, hatred, foolishness and idolatry in him before killing him along with all his sons.

Fear is no small business, it is a world of big evil when it comes from the wrong source (Satan).

The ten spies also took their eyes off God in Numbers 13 and at the end of the day, God wiped them out along with a good number of the Israelites.

Numbers 14:10 – 24, 28 – 29, 35 – 37.

See Numbers 14:11.

They took their eyes away from God and they did not recall to heart what God did in the past.

Consider Ruth the Moabite in Ruth 1:15 – 17.

Ruth must have seen God do marvelous things during those years she was still with her husband; Naomi's son, before his death. She must have heard a lot of the marvelous acts of God from the Israelite family into which she was married.

And so, when time came for Ruth to decide, she said she will not take her eyes off God, she held on to God – Yaweh Israel – while Orpah took her eyes off after a little persuasion.

SO, IN ACTUAL SENSE, FEAR STARTS WITH TAKING OUR EYES AWAY FROM GOD.

"See everything in life, *and* **fear sets in,** *but* **see only God,** *and* **fear trembles out."**

See Peter in Matthew 14:28-30.

The moment anything tries buying your attention from God, know for certain that that thing is a fear trap to knock you out.

This is really so because putting your eyes on God gives you the fear of God, but taking your eyes away from Him puts you in jeopardy of the fear of this evil world's dark prince, Satan, the one in charge of the world' system.

John 12:31, 14:30, 16:11; Ephesians 2:1 – 2.

So, if you do not want God's fear, Satan's fear is the only remaining option, no sitting on the fence at all in life.

CHAPTER 2

POSSIBILITIES WHEN FEAR BEGINS

Back to our text of Genesis 3:8-12, we want to consider verses 8,9,10, and 11 in detail.

In the concluding parts of chapter one, we saw that when we take our eyes, attention or focus away from God to other things, fear inevitably sets in. In this chapter it will interest you to know of some very brief possibilities – good ones – when fear is in the egg stage, that is, starting stages.

In verses 8 to 11 of Genesis chapter 3, some events took place that we will like the Holy Spirit to bring to our hearts. This, will help us understand the will of God, and keep us as " more than conquerors" just as God made us to be.

VERSE 8

In the early stage of fear, God does not cease to make His ways visible as He tries to reclaim the attention of the fearful.

What a loving and powerful heavenly father He is.

When you walk, movement is gradual, and so anyone watching you can see the dynamics of your moving legs easily.

While fear sets in, God begins to walk to give evidence of His ways to reclaim the focus of His beloveth: Adam and Eve. Even you and I.

They, Adam and Eve, hid because they sensed the steps they were hearing was coming towards them. This gives the picture that even in the state of that fear, God notices the fearful and still loves the fearful enough to move swiftly, but calmly, to begin to reveal His way to the fearful, in order to reclaim their attention.

See Matthew 14:26 – 31

The disciples had just seen what seemed like a ghost, and were afraid. They were not just afraid but they cried out in fear. You know that kind of shout we hear from children when they are scared. But as soon as they all, including Peter, cried out in fear, Jesus moved quickly with a loud voice, not a gentle voice, a voice loud enough to be heard, because everywhere was noisy. It was a rough and boisterous sea. Verse 24. It was a serious storm with winds and waves, and the disciples cried in fear. So Jesus had to shout so loud that they could hear Him and recognize His voice.

If Christ had not intervened to let them all know He was the one, I believe some of them would probably dive into the sea out of fear. Drowning would have being inevitable. So, in the state of their fear, Jesus spoke and got their eyes away from their fear and reclaimed their attention. This then gave Peter the courage to ask Jesus if he could also walk on the water. There is always a move by God in the midst of our fears to reclaim our focus, and attention.

Their fear of a ghost was overcome as Christ caught their attention. After reclaiming their attention, Peter, in his own eyes believed he had gotten it all worked out, yet his eyes were on the wind and the rough seas.

See a clearer picture of the incident here, the sea was very rough, probably worse than the roughness of the Atlantic Ocean, and yet Jesus walked on it. Peter saw this and made a move to do the same after receiving Jesus' permission, but ended up making only a little progress. Why?

The rough seas.

If the sea was calmer, probably he would have walked on it without drowning.

So long as that sea was rough, Peter kept seeing and focusing on it. He could see how the wind was blowing his garment and that of Jesus; how the wind blew their hair and beards. So his attention that was briefly captured by Jesus suddenly got lost again to the roughness of the sea and the winds. Immediately he lost sight of Jesus, fear of the seas set in again.

But the good news was that he soon gave his eyes and focus back to Jesus and cried out for help.

Peter, here, demonstrated that fear may come a second time even when conquered, but when we set our attention back on God He is always close by, trying to reclaim our attention to save us from the it.

Peter saw that while he was sinking, Jesus was standing firm; notwithstanding the rough sea and high winds. In the midst of all these, Peter saw the omnipotence of Jesus as Jesus kept walking towards him while he sank; just waiting for Peter to make the call for help. This is the same thing that was expected of Adam when he and his wife sinned against God.

Peter recognized the ways of God in Christ Jesus and asked for deliverance from his fears.

Matthew 14:32 reveals it quite uniquely; "...immediately they got into the boat, the wind ceased". This tells us that after Jesus saved Peter from the fear of drowning, Peter still walked on the rough sea in the midst of the high wind along with Jesus Christ. They both kept walking on the sea after Jesus pulled him up from the water(as he drowned), back on top of the water until they got into the boat. Peter had learnt his lessons so much that this time around, his attention remained on Jesus even though the sea was still rough and the wind high.

See the same verse in NLT (New Living Translation)

Matthew 14:32

"when they climbed back into the boat, the wind stopped."

This shows that Jesus did not carry Peter, Peter walked with Jesus back to the boat, and they entered into the boat together.

See, one great possibility in that fearful state is the way, and walk of God. He seeks, to have and reclaim your attention. This is what the Spirit of God is revealing.

Peter tried the impossible and sank when his eyes got distracted from Jesus, but he cried out and he was helped by the Lord. Jesus held his hands and pulled him up to stay on the same sea. If that fear has defeated you before, God is waiting for to cry out to Him as He desires to have your attention. He pulls you out and puts you back to ride on the same tide that would have drowned you. After He gained the attention of Moses at the burning bush, God placed him back on top of the things that he feared that made him run away 40 years ago. Wow!

Just as Peter walked with Jesus after he was rescued from his fears, in the same manner God walked with Moses after saving him from his fear. This is part of what can happen in that fear you face, it is a great opportunity to have God all for yourself to walk with you like never before.

One secret of Peter's life that is synonymous to King David's life, is that he always cried out early for help. I believe Peter's motto in life will be something like this: "If I can just be rescued, I will try again and never fear nor fail a second time." No wonder he was appointed for the big task of leading the church in its early stage.

Someone who did the contrary was King Saul.

I Samuel 10:21 – 24, 13:10 – 12, 15:24 – 26

Saul's fear never made him cry out to God for help. His eyes and ears refused to see or take notice of the ways of God. And as such, his attention was never reclaimed by God until fear sank and killed him with several more sins to his credit.

When you look intently into **Numbers 14:10 – 11**, God made a profound declaration in **verse 11**,

"Why is it that these people have refused to pay attention to the things I have being doing?"

God probably asked, "Didn't they go out early this morning to gather manna?" "That's enough sign."

"Can't they see the cloud up there under this hot desert sun that keeps them from the scorching heat? Are they not aware that the presence of the clouds I put in the sky above them is why the weather is conducive for them?" "Can't they see that I did that too?"

"Why then have they refused to see or notice me as I walk in their midst?"

God left them with signs every day; they saw all of these signs and yet refused to believe. That is why He was angry with them. "You fear mere men who can't give manna. You fear mere men who can't give the cloud in the sky to hide the heat of the sun from you. Don't you have eyes to see my signs and know my ways and be saved." But it all fell on deaf ears.

God have mercy!

Whenever fear sets in, you will see God walking, and His way becomes evident. Give your attention to that (His way) and let your attention stay on God rather than on the fear.

Please take these prayer points seriously.

1.   Father have mercy on my soul in Jesus name.

2.   I have sinned Lord, please forgive all my sins and restore me to Yourself in Jesus name.

3.   My heart, my soul, my all, I hand over to You forever in Jesus name.

4.   Father, I confess all my fears (*Go ahead and mention all the fears in your heart one by one*) to You.

5.   Father, You are bigger and mightier than... (*Mention each of those fears one at a time*). You are the greatest in Jesus name.

6.   Father, by the power in Jesus name I hand over all my fears to You now. I receive You in place of all the fears from now on in Jesus name.

7.   From today father, cause me to focus on only You and not on any fear again in Jesus name.

8.   Thank You my loving father for answering in Jesus name.

First possibility

You can still see God's ways, presence, as he calls your attention in the midst of fear. No matter how it might seem.

VERSE 9

"Then the LORD God called to Adam and said to him, 'where are you?' "

41

This, you will agree with me is a question. I believe you will also agree with me that the Lord God is all knowing, and all-surpassing in knowledge.

Now, a question:

As a sane person, can you take a beautiful painting and show a blind man and then ask:

"Hey, blind man, don't you see how beautiful this painting is?"

Or rather, you take a recording of a beautifully composed orchestra or any fine song, then you play that record before some deaf fellows and then ask them if they enjoyed the tracks.

Doing either of these will amount to you trying to mock them. That will not be acceptable by any sane thinking individual who sees you do such.

Now, if this is wrong and wicked by the standard of a right thinking society, how much more is it with God?

God will never do such, to make fun of a person's physical challenges.

If this is the case, it therefore implies that even in that condition of fear that Adam found himself or foolishly walked into, he could still hear voices. God knew Adam could still hear Him clearly and that is why God spoke to him.

In Matthew 14:26 – 27, in the midst of their fears, Jesus spoke out aloud to tell them He was the one. If the disciples were deaf and couldn't hear Jesus, Jesus wouldn't even say a thing, talk more of affirming His presence on the sea as He walked to them.

When you go through I Kings 19:2 – 12,

Even in the state of fear, Elijah could hear God clearly. He heard the angel, and also heard God. Even God's still small voice.

That is another positive possibility in the state of fear any child of God can have.

Even in the midst of fear God speaks, and when there is a speaking from God He expects a hearing from us. In Joshua 1:1 – 10, when Moses died and it was time for God to begin to tell Joshua what he should do, the first

things God told him after letting him know the task before him was: **"FEAR NOT"** verse 9.

"Be of good courage" verse 7.

Why was God talking in such a manner against fear while addressing Joshua? This is not farfetched from the fact that God could see the fear in Joshua.

Joshua probably had never envisaged taking over from Moses. He was just a humble servant following Moses and had no desire to take over. He never ever thought about it.

You have probably heard that proverb which says:

"Uneasy lies the head that wears the crown."

Well, Joshua never knew this proverb until it was time to take over.

Joshua had being a man of faith who held on to God and believed he can conquer the Canaanites through the help of God and occupy the land. Yes he never lost faith in that, but what probably became Joshua's fears were the very people he was meant to lead.

I believe these thoughts probably ran through Joshua's mind:

"These people stressed Moses till he couldn't make it to the Promised Land, will I make it?"

- "Even Moses' brother and sister rebelled against him. Won't I face worse?"

- "They almost stoned Moses at several points, what will they do to me?'

These and many more questions I believe ran through his mind to scare him.

It was in the midst of these and many more analysis in his head that God came to interrupt his thoughts with these words:

1.   Verse 1. "Moses my servant is dead." "Joshua, know for certain that Moses was my own servant." This must have boosted Joshua's courage.

2.   Verse 3. "Joshua, you just walk on that place, that land and it shall be yours." "If your leg can just touch it then it's yours." Another booster. "That's easy" Joshua must have told himself by now.

3.   Verse 5. "No man can stand before you all your days just as they could not overcome Moses." Wow!

4.   Verse 5. "I will not leave you nor forsake you". I could just imagine Joshua shout; "at last". "That's all I just needed; Your presence."

5.   Verse 6. "You'll be the one to distribute the land to the people."

6.   Verse 6 – 8. "The secret for your success and conquest is this book of the law. That's the only work."

7.   Verse 9. "I God, I'm the one commanding you." Joshua's spirit must have fully revived by now. "So it's not an angel talking to me, it's Elohim Himself." Joshua was fully strong in spirit by now.

8.   Verse 9. "Do not fear. Just be bold."

We see what Joshua did next. Immediately he heard all the charge and address from God. Joshua moved into action quickly, no waste of time Joshua 1:10.

You see, in our fears, God speaks and we always hear Him. He speaks not to amaze with how powerful His voice is but to distract our attention from that fear and to bring us to Himself. To reclaim our hearts.

God spoke and by the time He was through, Joshua gave unwavering attention to God.

In Matthew 14:27 – 28, Jesus spoke and Peter's fear of seeing a ghost was immediately drowned as Peter became courageous and stepped out of the boat to walk on the water in faith.

Genesis 3:9 under consideration;

"...called to Adam and said..."

When we say you call out to a person, it means you shout out the person's name, not to scare, but to get their undivided attention. See, in the fearful state God specializes in calling out to us in a way that should be followed by giving Him our full attention. That is, God could get louder now with His tone just to get our attention.

In Luke 22:31, Christ called out to Peter twice to get his attention.

The essence of calling out to Adam was to draw his attention away from himself and bring him back to God, but Adam was lost in himself. Self-realization at best keeps one lost in self and destroys at the end of the day.

See (I Kings 19:9)

God came to Elijah and said to him; "what are you doing here, Elijah?"

This can only mean that this is not where God has placed him. "Elijah, why are you here?" The fear in Elijah had so affected him at this point that his response was not pleasing to God, so God had to ask the same question a second time;

I Kings 19:12 – 13

His response to God was still not pleasing to the Lord. The answer he gave to God twice was the reason God had to tell him to handover to three different people that will finish what was meant for him alone to accomplish.

I Kings 19:15 – 17. Such a mighty man of God carrying the office of two kings and two prophets (Elisha's double portion anointing were all in Elijah.)

Let us examine the response he gave.

I Kings 19:10

"So he said, I have been very zealous for the LORD God of hosts; for the children of Israel have forsaken Your covenant, torn down Your altars, and killed Your prophets with the sword. I alone am left; and they seek to take my life. " Verse 14 records the same response.

Question Again:

"Elijah what are you doing here?" Verses 9 and 13

"What are you doing here?" But in responding, due to the fears in his heart, Elijah's answers were only about the evils that the Israelites had committed, especially on God's altar, God's covenant and God's prophets.

In his response, the places we see Elijah make reference to himself was in praising himself for a job well done and how it had endangered his life.

"Elijah what are you doing here?"

His fear got him also confused as we saw in chapter one.

PRAY

• **Father, deliver me from any fear that will make me give a wrong answer to You in Jesus name.**

See the response again

Verse 10 and 14

"I have been very zealous for the LORD God of hosts... I alone am left; and they seek to take my life."

This is what Elijah actually meant;

"No other prophet of Yours has being as zealous as me, and I alone remain, yet the people want to kill me. If they do, You'll have no more prophets."

How wrong he was.

I Kings 19:18

What was the beginning of his fear?

It was not really Jezebel or her letter in verse 2, rather, Elijah had taken his eyes off God and was consumed by his zeal for God as a prophet. His thoughts: "Wow, seems I'm greater than all the prophets; Moses, Samuel. I have achieved so much."

I Kings 19:4

"... Take my life, for I am no better than my fathers!"

When attention shifts from God, fear sets in as stated, yet when God speaks to us in that state of fear, He expects a right response not just any answer. May we find divine help to speak rightly to God when facing fears in the name of Jesus.

A second possibility when fear combats us is God speaking audibly to the fearful in a bid to gain their attention. Isaiah 6:5 – 7

Prophet Isaiah both saw and heard and it drowned the fears he had about his sins.

VERSE 10

"… 'I heard Your voice in the gardens, and I was afraid because I was naked; and I hid myself.'"

One beautiful thing that is possible in our fearful state is God coming into where we really are. Not talking from far, but coming right where we are.

"…the LORD God walking in the garden…" verse 8

"…'I heard Your voice in the garden…'" verse 10

God comes right into the situation or scene of our fear.

First he makes His way, steps visible.

Second He speaks out to us to know we are not alone.

Then He is right there in it with us.

Look at it better here;

Isaiah 63:9 "In all their affliction He was afflicted, And the Angel of His presence saved them; In His love and in His pity He redeemed them; And He bore them and carried them all the days of old."

While in the garden of fear, God is right there too and not far away.

Hebrews 2:14 – 15, 18

"In as much then as the children have partaken of flesh and blood, He Himself likewise shared in the same, that through death He might destroy him who had the power of death, that is the devil, and release those who through fear of death were all their lifetime subject to bondage....For in that he Himself has suffered, being tempted, He is able to aid those who are tempted."

This is the description here;

Songs of Solomon 5:2 – 6

In her closet, her beloved came to her, right where she was and sought her. He was not far away calling out, but right where she was. In the very situation she found herself, there he came. This was exactly what God did for Adam; He came right where Adam was hidden/lost due to his fear.

Now hear what her beloveth says:

Songs of Solomon 5:2 – 6

Verse 2. "...'Open for me, my sister, my love, my dove, my perfect one; for my head is covered with dew, my locks with the drops of the night.'"

More like:

"Let me come to you, my head (my mind) is full of you and I sense your fear. I can see the dread in you, allow me to get to you."

It is similar to the way God came right where Adam was, in his fear.

Hear the response.

Verse 3. "I have taken off my robe; how can I put it on again? I have washed my feet; how can I defile them?"

Listening to this response, let me ask;

If he is your beloved - your husband - is there any need of putting back the robe? Who else is her nakedness meant for? It is for him.

That is no excuse at all.

"I have washed my feet, how can I defile them?"

This is better read as she saying she is lost in herself and self-pity, so she'll rather remain where she is than open up and be helped.

When God came to Adam and Adam told God he was hiding (in the wrong answer he gave), God could not do much for him that day. And so the help (salvation) Adam would have gotten that day was postponed for thousands of years.

He came right where she was just as God came right where Adam was and the response was not good enough.

Verse 4. "My beloved put his hand by the latch of the door, and my heart yearned for him."

As you already know, *a latch is a small metal bar that is used to fasten a door or a gate. You raise it to open the door, and drop it into a metal hook to fasten it.*

That is a latch.

This same verse in NLT reads;

"My lover tried to unlatch the door, my heart thrilled within me"

This means he tried to remove the obstacles on his path to reach out and help her. At this point she could see the efforts of her beloveth, yet she remained where she was hidden.

Even though by now she was relaxed to converse with him because he came in a gentle way, yet she shut herself in; "...and my heart thrilled within me"

When God came to Adam where he was hiding, God approached him in such a way that should not scare him, but Adam hid in self-pity and his fear. God tried unlocking the door since Adam will not. God employed several methods to help him open up; Adam remained hidden and unwilling to let the door open.

How did God try unlocking the door, that is, unlatching?

• By His ways, steps, walk to them not to agitate them.

• By His call in a gentle way. He called out in a way to make Adam approach Him. In a way that could make Adam think God does not even know I am naked.

- By coming to Adam right in his fearful condition.

- By the way God asked His question in verse 11 of Genesis 3

1. "Who told you that you were naked?"

2. "Have you eaten from the tree of which I commanded you that you should not eat?"

All these moves from the Almighty was just to unlatch the door for Him to gain full access to them and help them out. Yet, like the lady in S.O.S 5:2 – 6, Adam did not open up.

Verse 5 – 6 of S.O.S 5

By the time she was through with herself and ready to open, it was too late as the beloveth had gone.

For Adam, since he will not own up but was busy blaming everyone in his bid to justify himself, God could not do what He intended to do for him immediately, He

just covered his nakedness with the skin of the slain lamb and cover his sin with the blood of that slain lamb.

The fear that made him hide stole everything from him.

Back in childhood days I remember denying wrongs done out of fear of possible punishment. Many times though I was rebuked. The punishments came only when it was necessary to keep me in the right path in life. This, I believe was Adam's thought.

Adam had a lot that was going on in his mind. Things his heart told him God would do to him if he owned up.

Like the prodigal son in Luke 15:11 − 24, the day he returned was the day he received his mercy and redemption. If he had returned home earlier he would have received it earlier. Same was for Adam. I strongly believe if his fear had not gotten the better side of him and hid him away from God, he would have received help since that day.

See Isaiah's approach to it; Isaiah 6:1 – 8

After the demise of king Uzziah of Judah, God came to Isaiah right where he was, in his filthy self-righteousness. God caught Isaiah's attention and made an

announcement of His presence to him just as He did to Adam and that lover lady in Songs of Solomon.

But see how Isaiah responded; Isaiah 6:5

"So I said: woe is me, for I am undone! Because I am a man of unclean lips, And I dwell in the midst of a people of unclean lips; For my eyes have seen the king; The LORD of hosts."

Isaiah quickly seized the opportunity to confess he is a sinful man.

Isaiah did this in fear. Not just fear of God, but fear that he was a sinner. Just as Adam also became scared by reason of the knowledge of his sin. But Isaiah had a better approach to it. He owned up to it, went on to declare where and on whom his attention or focus has now turned.

Isaiah 6:5 "...I am a man of unclean lips;...I dwell in the midst of a people of unclean lips;..."

These were Isaiah's initial focus; himself and the people among whom he dwelt. But at that divine visit, Isaiah's attention quickly shifted to God.

Isaiah 6:5

- "...For my eyes have seen the King,..."

- "...The LORD of hosts."

Isaiah was just saying the one whom my attention is now totally fixed on is the King, not a king but the King.

The one I focus on is The LORD of hosts.

Isaiah quickly acknowledged the magnanimity of the one he was now seeing and this gave birth to a response from him which he declared loudly.

I could just imagine God declare, "Just what I was expecting from Adam. Good response Isaiah"

In the remaining part of this encounter, you will discover that the very things he feared were dealt with by God immediately. The sins he feared were atoned for immediately. Even without him requesting for it.

Just imagine Adam responding outside of fear, there would have being help there and then to deal with the fear, the sin. Remember, God is no respecter of persons.

Isaiah 6:7 "...Behold, this has touched your lips; your iniquity is taken away, and your sin purged (atoned for)."

Take note of this, in all our fears, God comes in by Himself, all He needs is for you to take your eye away from that fear and place your full attention on Him so He can help you out of that fear.

Thirdly, in the state of fear, God is present and not far away. Psalm 46:1

VERSE 11

The ways of God, the voice of God and the full presence of God are the initial possibilities in that state of fear. As we move on, we want analyze verse 11 of Genesis 3, to consider questions like: Who are you listening to? What did I do to get here?

These are issues that constitute part of the possibilities in the early phases of fear.

Genesis 3:11

"...who told you...?" Have you eaten from the tree...?'"

"Who told you?"

These are the questions,

Who are you listening to?

The truth about life is that what you keep feeding on will determine your state of health. This also applies to your state of mind. Psychologists advise parents to encourage their children from young age because it helps them believe in themselves and make them reach out for excellence as they grow. This is because words are powerful.

Job 4:4

Even the brave David at some points got scared.

I Samuel 21:10 – 12

See what verse 11 says;

"'And the servants of Achish said to him, "Is this not David the king of the land? Did they not sing of him to one another in dances, saying: 'Saul has slain his thousands, And David his ten thousands?"

David, at the time this conversation was going on between Achish and his servants, was privy to hear what was going on and it stirred great fear in him. David, being a man of war and leader of people knows that you do not lose the opportunity to apprehend the enemy

who slew your soldiers, so he feared for his life. I Samuel 21:12

"Now David took these words to heart, and was very much afraid of Achish the king of Gath."

David heard the words, and he took it to heart, and that produced the fear that chased him out of Gath to Adullam. I Samuel 21:13 – 22:1

Why was God particular about the question He first asked Adam when Adam told Him of his predicament?

"And He said, 'who told you that you were naked?'" Genesis 3:11

This is because no matter who you are, the person you listen to is the one that gets your full attention. And if you listen to yourself a lot, certainly you will place your attention on yourself. If you listen to the devil, you will surely focus your attention on him. But if your ears are given to God, certainly you will listen to Him, and He will get your full attention.

God was invariably telling Adam; "I now see why you are afraid. You have being listening to someone else and you have disregarded my own voice. And that has gotten your attention, little wonder fear has set in."

See what James has to say concerning what you hear, or rather, who you listen to.

James 3:3 – 8

James is saying here that, the tongue is the steering that controls lives. Verse 3 and 4

As small as the tongue is, it controls the whole life of a person. This means then that the tongue you listen to is the tongue that gets your attention, and that is the tongue that rules your life.

God's tongue, or other tongues.

Take special note of the point here. *In the time of fear many voices speak, basically two voices; God and Satan's, and you will surely listen to one, there is no sitting on the fence. Whichever you listen to plays a vital role; to nurse the fear and remain in it, or hate the fear and come out of it.*

That is one of the reasons God spoke to Adam in his state of fear when the fear came on him.

Please think on this scenario in I Samuel 4:2 – 10

Israel faced the Philistines in a battle, and prior to this battle the Philistines had consistently dealt heavy

defeats on the Israelites, and so the Philistine soldiers came to this particular war fully hopeful and convinced they will defeat Israel effortlessly. The Philistines came with so much confidence.

On the other hand Israel came to this battle with so much fear. See verse 2 – 3.

Their fear led them to take a drastic decision to bring out the Ark of covenant to the battle.

Immediately the Ark was brought into the camp of the Israelite soldiers, a noise went forth, so loud that the Philistine soldiers became terrified. The shout sent shivers into their spine. The once bold Philistine soldiers suddenly became afraid. Why?

Because at this point, another voice had overshadowed the initial voice of confidence that they had. I Samuel 4:6 – 8

Just like Adam who all of a sudden forgot the voice of God; the voice of courage. The Philistines also forgot the sounds, and voices of courage that ushered them to the battle and this nursed fear in them.

This is similar to when God had to ask Adam, "Who told you that you were naked?" that is, who have you been listening to?

The Philistines would have become mincemeat for Israel had they began the battle with this fear. See what happened in verse 9 (I Samuel 4)

"Be strong and conduct yourselves like men, you Philistines that you do not become servants of the Hebrews, as they have been to you. Conduct yourselves like men, and fight!"

To save the situation from degenerating, this encouragement from one of the captains or commandants became a great booster; this was another voice the Philistines later heard. This second voice countered that of the Hebrews. This captain first discovered courage in himself and went on to spread it. The voice of courage in the midst of fear could silence any fear.

Someone in the ranks of the Philistines got up, managed his fear, dismissed its voices, got his ears opened to that of courage and then dug out the evil seed of fear from the hearts of his comrades through his own voice.

Who do you listen to?

... A doctor who tells you that you cannot be healed, and you will just have to manage an ailment all your life or

God who says "Come unto me all ye that labor and are heavy laden and I will give you rest."

... Friends who say you will certainly fail or God who says, "You can do all things through Christ that strengthens you."

... The scary weather report or financial report?

In I Samuel 30:6 – 8, David heard the voices of distress and fear that would have taken him to his early grave with his destiny unfulfilled. In this circumstance, David summoned up the warrior's heart in him and threw away his fears and encouraged himself in the Lord. He quickly gave his ear to God and closed his ears against the contrary voices speaking. See verse 6b

"...But David strengthened himself in the Lord his God."

The time you need to be most careful who you listen to is when you sense fears around. At this point, many voices will be busy telling you how naked you are, and this will certainly overcome you if your attention is not turned from them.

Listen rather to the voice telling you that you can be clothed again. You can stand again.

"Adam! Who told you that you were naked?"

The second question was.

What did I do to get here?

Genesis 3:11

"...have you eaten from the tree of which I commanded you that you should not eat?"

In Physics there is a principle known as **CAUSE AND EFFECT.** This says, for every action, there is a resultant reaction.

For example, if I hit my right fist against a wall, there will be both sound, and pain. Sound of the collision, as well as pain in my hand due to the forceful collision.

For Adam, the cause that produced an effect was eating of the forbidden fruit. This act is synonymous to him excusing himself from focusing on God.

Remember, we established earlier in chapter 1 that what we focus on, is what determines the presence or absence of the kind of fear we are considering.

Adam's way of initially shifting his attention from God was the forbidden fruit. While for Job, it was setting his heart on his self-righteousness, his wealth and fear of losing it. Job 3:25 – 26

Looking at Job 3:10 – 24, we notice some salient points that were sources of fear for Job;

- Verse 10. Fear of having sorrow

- Verse 13. Fear of losing his rest – comfort

- Verse 17 & 18. Fear of being troubled and oppressed.

So what actually did Job do that brought these fear upon him?

His eyes were on himself. Job thought was able to attain righteous standing before God by his personal works and ability.

Job 1:5 is a proof of this presumption.

Besides, in his arguments with his three friends; Eliphaz the Temanite, Bildad the Shuhite, and Zophar the Naamathite, Job justified himself over and over again. Unknown to him, our righteousness is like filthy rags before God. Isaiah 64:6

Let's take a look at some of Job's defense and his show of self-righteousness that brought this fears.

In Job 4:17, Eliphaz pointed out to Job his error of equating himself with God and setting himself more righteous than God by the question he asked.

In Job 6:24, Job gave an answer. Still justifying himself. More like he asking; "In what way have I done any wrong?", "I have checked my self and there is no uncleanness." That's the basis of what Job was affirming.

Still focusing on himself, Job in Job 7:20 queried God "why", believing that he was clean and without offence.

Another instance of setting his eyes on himself is

Job 9:21 – 22. Here, Job actually told God; "I now see that you destroy even the blameless man because that is what you are doing to me now."

Take a close look at Job 10:2 – 7.

What Job was expected to actually do was to take a good thought and know what had transpired that probably got him to this situation, but instead, his self-praise and self-justification continued.

Job 13:18 – 23

Job had even prepared arguments to bring against God. To also let God know how wrong and unjust He had treated him (the self-righteous Job).

Job 27:2 – 6 shows clearly what we are trying to say. Job said:

• God has taken away justice. Verse 2. God is unrighteous.

• I have done no evil, I am righteous.

• I will never accept any word that condemns me. I cannot be condemned; "I rather die than accept that I am unrighteous". Verse 5 – 6.

• I will never forsake my self-righteousness (which is filthy rags before God. Isaiah 64:6) verse 6.

Job was so consumed with himself he could not see God at all.

See Job 31:1 – end.

In this chapter of the book of Job, we see Job at the height of his self-acclaimed purity and right standing. From verse 1 to verse 40, Job's concentration was on 'I'; self. He narrated many times the good he had done, and the evils and wrongs he never did.

Job 31:33 shows his pride of not being unrighteous as he compared himself with all others. He assumed he was better than others as far as he was concerned.

Let us see how he was finally addressed in his self-righteous aggrandizement.

Job 32:1

This verse summarizes it all. Whenever a person is unable to correctly answer questions on how he got to this place of fear, then help is impossible or difficult.

Adam could not give the correct answers, he excused himself. Job also could not, he justified himself.

All of Job's answers and replies kept his eyes away from God but on himself, and that is the starting point of fear as we said. His fears continued until the young man Elihu spoke and when God Himself also spoke. Job 32:2

It is whom your attention is fixed on that you praise. From the beginning of his fear to this point Job's eyes were on himself and not on God.

His arguments and replies showed where Job's attention had been: "Won't this all powerful God still decide to judge me one day even with all my righteousness."

God's response later came in order to correct Job:

Job 40:1 – 5, 8.

Verse 8 "Would you indeed annul My judgment? Would you condemn Me that you may be justified?"

"Job!" God must have called out, "would you fix your eyes on yourself and your self-righteousness while you disdain Me and not look at Me at all to see Me in My full splendor and true righteousness?"

Job at this point must have been terrified. At this point, fear was changing its form. It was becoming the fear of God. To help Job take his eyes and attention off himself and put them back on God, God began to list just a little of His deeds, I call this, part of God's Curriculum Vitae or God's Résumé .

Job 40:9 – 41:1 – 34.

Finally Job got the point and gave a true answer to what he did that brought him to that level of fear.

Job 42:1 – 6.

- Verse 2. "I know you are able always"

- Verse 3. "I have being foolish and wrong in my responses."

- Verse 5. "Now I can see You clearly. I cease to see myself anymore." More like, finally; "I see my filthiness and Your righteousness."

- Verse 6. "I am nothing at all, and I amount to nothing, You are all."

- Verse 6. "I repent." Wow!

These were the very things God was waiting to hear from Adam and help him. The curses on the earth and the negative decree on the woman during child birth would have been averted.

Can I sincerely answer that question?

Will you?

What did I do to get here?

David probably answered his in

I Samuel 30:6 by telling himself, "I set my eyes on the battle with the Philistines and never set my eyes on God to ask for a Yes or No." David corrected this early.

In Matthew 14:29 – 31, Peter answered correctly; "my eyes were not set on Jesus." But when he realized this and focused on Jesus, his fears ended immediately as Jesus stretched forth His hands and pulled him up out of the water.

Esther 4:1 – 17, in seeking to deliver the Hebrews who were her people, Esther's eyes were initially focused on the king and that gave her fears.

Verse 11

"All the king's servants and the people of the king's provinces know that any man or woman who goes into the inner court to the king, who has not been called, he has but one law: put all to death, except the one to whom the king holds out the golden scepter, that he may live. Yet I myself have not been called to go in to the king these thirty days."

Esther's initial idea was if only my husband, the king, will invite me to the inner court, I would petition him. This focus only got her scared. But by the time Mordechai's reply got to her, Esther had to change her focus to "the hills from whence cometh her help". Verse 15 – 16.

The change of focus to whom she gave her attention to suddenly drowned her fears and gave her boldness to approach the king. That enabled her to achieve her desire. Psalm 121:1 & 2.

Some may have their attention on themselves like Job, others may have their attention on another person, and some others may have their own attention on things, on reports and the present systems. Just make sure your attention is on God.

KNOWLEDGE AND FEAR

How does knowledge or what you know affect fear. Or what role does knowledge play in relation to fear? Genesis 3:7 – 8.

When we take a study of the cases of fears that people had, it is undeniable that knowledge played a vital role in breeding the fear.

Verse 7 and 10 of Genesis chapter 3 clearly points this out. Verse 7 says "...and they knew that they were naked,..."

Verse 10 says "...and I was afraid because I was naked; and I hid myself."

You will agree with me that; "they knew" meant they obtained knowledge. They had knowledge that they were naked. Out of this knowledge of their nakedness proceeded forth their fears. The example of Adam in verse 10.

Recent knowledge about red meat and carbonated drinks have gone a long way in making a lot of people redefine their intake of these things. Knowledge is indeed powerful.

Knowledge works hand in hand with fear.

Depending on the kind of knowledge though.

II Samuel 3:6 – 11.

After King Saul's death, his minister of defence, that is, his chief of staff Abner made sure that Saul's son, Ishbosheth, became king. After a while Ishbosheth wrongly accused Abner of having an affair with Rizpah king Saul's concubine. This so provoked Abner that he confronted Ishbosheth and made him know that because of the wrong accusation, he will hand over the kingdom to David and make sure David becomes king.

Being fully aware of Abner's position and power, Ishbosheth began to be afraid. This new development made Ishbosheth scared.

That is knowledge for you.

Just like the incident that happened to Elijah in

I Kings 19:1 - 3.

The knowledge of what Jezebel had done to all the prophets of God was still fresh in Elijah's heart coupled with the knowledge of the threats of Jezebel to deal with him. All these contributed to the fears in Elijah's life, so much that he fled for his life.

What you decide to know can become the beginning of fear if you permit it.

In I Samuel 28:4 – 5, when Saul knew how many soldiers came from the Philistines to fight Israel, he got afraid. Besides, in the book of Numbers 13:1 – 14:1, when the twelve spies that were sent to spy the land of Canaan returned, ten out of the twelve had a negative report that they brought while only two brought another report: positive.

The negative report of the ten gave a wrong knowledge to the people. The negative knowledge succeeded in giving all the Hebrews fear instead of courage.

"I might not have being there to experience it, see it or hear it, but the knowledge I acquire from another person about it may breed fear or faith."

On the issue relating to fear, you need to be careful with those who give you information or knowledge. It could be true that the little child is sick, but another person will give you this knowledge in a way that gives you the hope of a positive change of things later, while another will give the same report in a way that can make you believe that the child will not live beyond the next minute. This second report certainly breeds fear. Fear kills faster than illness.

See this example in Galatians 2:11- 14.

We see in this verses how the knowledge of the presence of a sect of the circumcision at Antioch brought fear into Peter's heart, and in turn Peter's ways of doing things changed, by reason of this fear.

Dynamics of fear

Peter was once bold to eat with the uncircumcised, but immediately he knew some of the sect of the circumcision from Jerusalem were around, Peter feared and acted hypocritically.

I Samuel 4:7- 8. These Philistines were not there, nor were even their grandfathers the period in history that God dealt with the gods of Egypt and the Egyptians. Yet they heard about it over the years from generation to generation and it became knowledge to them. Little wonder when they learnt that God was now in the Hebrews' camp (the Ark amidst a camp of sinful Israel), they were so scared. They recalled with good knowledge what God did for Israel in the past. It took another form of knowledge that came from a Philistine to conquer this fear.

Remember the definition of fear:

"The bad feeling that you get when you are in danger, when something bad might happen, or when a particular thing frightens you."

From this definition, we can draw out a strong point that knowledge or experience is what gives you the definition of danger.

What do I mean by this?

Nothing is considered dangerous to me except what experience has taught me about that thing. The experience may be what I was actually involved in or what I witnessed another person being involved in. In some cases, some things will not be considered dangerous by me except if knowledge teaches me so.

For instance;

I was on a commercial motor bike somewhere in Jos, Plateau state, Nigeria sometime in august, 2008. In my bid to arrive where I was going on time, I told the driver to speed up. This landed us both in an accident. I did not arrive there because the journey was truncated by the accident. It was by the mercies of God we survived.

Later, as I analyzed the whole incident, I realized my instruction to the driver to speed up caused the accident. The driver was initially moving at his own pace: a speed he could easily manage. I had told him to do what he could not.

This taught me never to tell anyone to increase speed while driving as they might just be driving at their own

speed limits, except though if I know the fellow is a fast driver.

Besides, knowledge or experience tells us how dangerous an un-insulated live electric cable could be to the human body if high voltage electricity is running through it. This is what makes us keep it away from where children are. At a tender age they do not know the dangers and may go near to play with it, but as adults, the knowledge of what it can do gets us to keep them away.

So, knowledge of what is considered dangerous to me is what works out that feeling I get when I am said to be in fear. Without the knowledge of that danger, I will not fear.

In Elijah's case: I Kings 19:1 – 3, part of his fears came on him because he had knowledge of what Jezebel had done to people like himself (Prophets.)

I Kings 19:10,14

"And he said, 'I have been very zealous for the Lord God of hosts; because the children of Israel have… and killed Your prophets with the sword…' "

I Kings 18:4, 13.

The equation will look something like this to Elijah:

God's prophets + Jezebel = Dead prophets.

A dangerous irreversible equation.

For Elijah it was not just an equation but reality facing him head on.

So, while his eyes went on himself, the reality of the danger also began to dawn on him to poison him. This fear later led him to flee.

Hear this:

"Fear builds on the foundation of knowledge, Give fear no knowledge of danger and a heart will laugh at what is actually dangerous"

See how God proves this point to Job in His discourse with him.

Job 39:19 – 25. A very accurate description of what happens in the heart of a horse in battle is given to us by God Almighty Himself who created the horse.

Normally, no one else knows a product better than the one who created or produced the product. Be it electronics or automobiles. Also, living creatures.

Verse 21b "...He gallops into the clash of arms."

Verse 22"He mocks at fear, and is not frightened; Nor does he turn back from the sword."

Why does the horse mock, that is, disdain fear as stated by God Himself? Allow me to show you. It is because the knowledge of the danger of war or battle is hidden from it. And since it lacks this knowledge, the horse charges on into the battle until it either survives or dies in it.

A dog will not even go that far before it flees.

Have you considered it or probably you have experienced it, the same horse that mocks at fear in battle is the same horse that will definitely flee with speed at the sight of a snake; no matter how small the snake may be. Why? The knowledge of the dangers of a snake is given to it.

An eagle on the other hand will rather tactically attack and kill a snake than run from it. Why? Knowledge.

What we are driving at is this: when the knowledge of a dangerous thing or happening is lacking in you; or you view the knowledge of any danger as not dangerous at all, you will definitely not bow to fear when confronted with that thing.

I marvel when I watch real life documentaries on DISCOVERY CHANNEL, I see people catch crocodiles, or even enter lion's dens.

Amazing. These people are well aware of the dangers of these wild, yet they go to them because they have

silenced any fear knowledge related to these wild beasts.

Beware of danger and nurse fear, or cast out the dangers and courage sets in.

Not presumption but consciously working on it.

I am not a horse that naturally has no knowledge of any danger nor am I an Ostrich that naturally lacks knowledge of dangers as Job 39:13 – 17 says. Well, you are neither a horse nor an Ostrich and that is why that knowledge of danger must be changed.

That wrong knowledge of danger can become a thing of the past.

Nehemiah 6:5 – 9

When you read the earlier chapters of the book of Nehemiah, you will be introduced to some fellows who had Sanballat as their main gang leader. Right from the beginning of the work that Nehemiah was doing in Jerusalem, these people did all they could to stop the work. Many tactics and gimmicks were employed yet all failed.

Nehemiah 2:10, 19

The enemy used reproach, insults, shame, and mockery to try to stop the work but Nehemiah remained strong.

Nehemiah 4:1 says.

"But it so happened, when Sanballat heard that we were rebuilding the wall that he was furious and very indignant, and mocked the Jews."

"…and mocked the Jews."

Next we see that as reproach, disgrace, insults were not achieving anything against the builders of the walls, Sanballat and his hosts resorted to violence. To attack. Nehemiah 4:7 – 13.

Verse 8. "And all of them conspired together to come and attack Jerusalem and create confusion."

So, we see the enemy fight them with mockery, and insults and disgrace. When this failed they went violent, but it failed also because Nehemiah foiled it by taking precautionary measures.

The point therefore from all these is this, that Sanballat and his hosts decided to finally use fear when the first two tactics failed. Nehemiah 6:5-9

Verse 9. "For they all were trying to make us afraid, saying, 'their hands will be weakened in the work, and it will not be done.' Now therefore, O God strengthen my hands."

Verse 5 to 8 gives a detail of the letter (**knowledge**) they brought to Nehemiah's awareness in order to create fear. See Nehemiah 5:10 – 14

Fear was introduced again through a form of knowledge. This time around, the knowledge took the form of prophecies (**satanic prophecies I call them**). Nehemiah being strengthened by God could not be defeated by this either.

Kenneth Haggin, one of the fathers of faith once said: **"you can't stop a bird from flying over your head but you can stop it from perching on your head."**

What a very accurate truth. Knowledge will keep prowling around, in and out of your ear, but it is left for you to disgrace it out or allow it to land and perch.

You can help yourself. Stop visiting places where they feed you with the wrong knowledge. It is not all that the media has to say that is really the truth; the media is well monitored by a few and they control people's lives using this tool, be careful too.

Besides, also know that knowledge and fear work vice versa.

What do I mean?

A form of knowledge works fear, and that fear goes on to implement another knowledge. For instance:

The fear of hunger leads some to steal. That is, the dangers of being famished can cause people to apply the knowledge of stealing.

Matthew 6:25 – 27,31 & I Timothy 6:9 says worrying is a form of fear.

One definition of worry is this:

"To keep thinking about unpleasant things that might happen or about problems that you have."

Worrying is a fruit of fear. It is one of the signs of fear. And that is one reason Jesus kicked against it, and Apostle Paul went on to tell Timothy how the knowledge that breeds the fear of worry can lead people into acting on many other negative knowledge at their disposal and end up captives (ensnared). They end up indulging in harmful knowledge that will eventually destroy them.

Worry is what leads men to keep wanting more and more until they follow the wrong, evil knowledge to achieve it.

Fear, is really dangerous

I want to tell you, a good number, not all, of the people who fell into one evil enterprise or the other all started from fear of something. This fear certainly came through a form of knowledge they were privy to.

Note this:

Knowledge is the ground on which fear thrives. Put out the knowledge that is causing that fear and you will kill the feelings of danger, then fear dies.

Let us conclude this chapter with this.

Growing up as a young child I used to like a very popular carbonated soft drink. But over the years as a young man, so much knowledge about the danger of that drink began to proliferate: "its high sugar content", "its chemical composition", and many other comments about its harmful content. Most scary was how it was said that the drink can even be used as toilet bowl stain remover.

These knowledge made me gradually see the drink as dangerous. Within the shortest period of time every like for the drink waned in me.

The truth is, that soft drinks had probably always been like that all the years I craved it and enjoyed it. But since no knowledge of its danger came to me, drinking it did not bother me until the knowledge came.

This is similar to how knowledge works to create fear.

PRAY

1.   Lord Jesus, in Your name I renounce every knowledge that breeds fear in me in Jesus name.

2.   I decree: all of my heart, my soul, my mind I submit to only the knowledge of Jesus Christ the son of God in Jesus name.

CHAPTER 4

SIGNS OF FEAR: STAGES IN FEAR

Fear does certainly come with proofs that it exists and that it is at work. These signs will be revealed to us to help us stand our guard in the future.

Ever seen a child that is afraid of the dark? If possible, that child can scream down a building if left alone in the dark.

Besides, things in nature do not just spring up from nowhere, they go through stages till they get to maturity. So does fear. It has stages. It occurs in stages.

And if quickly recognized at its earliest stage and dealt with, it will never grow to become a stubborn rooted plant in our lives. During my early years as a believer in Christ Jesus, I heard a lot about divine healing and I desired it. I heard a lot of teachings on it. The teachings did little good until I listened to a series of teachings by Andrew Wommack on divine healing. From his teachings on divine healing, I learnt to deal with sicknesses immediately I sense it approaching my body. Don't tell me you can't tell when sickness is trying to get your body! From his teaching, I learnt not to leave an approaching sickness to get control of me, when I can stop it from maturing to the point of weakening my body. Right from that point of acquiring knowledge, I'd rather deal with an approaching ill health immediately I sense strange signs in my body like: high temperature of my breath, or when my joints begin to ache, or any other strange changes in my body that could be sickness related than leave it to mature and take control of my body.

This teachings helped me to easily deal with any sickness early enough to stop it from developing roots and becoming full grown when much faith will then be required to fight it. At the seed stage, it is easier dealing with things. This has worked very well for me.

This makes it important to know the stages of fear and to also know the seed stage in order to be able to fight it early before it develops. Fear starts gradually.

What I am trying to say is that signs and stages work hand in hand. For instance, before a sickness knocks a person down, except in very rare cases, it starts with some signs like the breath getting warmer, lack of appetite, joint aches, headaches, nausea etc.

These signs develop and later manifest as full blown ailment. The signs clearly reveal the stage.

Another example could be pregnancy. The signs reveal the stages of development of the growing foetus in the womb.

So, basically, signs show how a new development is going on and in turn tells of the stage or level that the development is at. When you read Matthew 24:1 – 40, in detailing the signs of His return and of the end times, Jesus called the first signs as; "first of the birth pains." (NLT) verse 8 "But all this is only the first of the birth pains, with more to come."

After the first signs, verse 1 – 8, Jesus continued and spoke of other signs from verse 9 to 28 (NKJV)

These signs He described thus:

"Wherever the carcass is, there the eagles will be gathered together."

Signs are quite important in life because they point to a stage that is in operation. As the sign changes it shows a proof that that stage is over and a new one will begin.

So, the signs of fear and the stages of fear work hand in hand. The signs reveal there is a stage of fear at work. As the signs increase in intensity, it reveals that the stage of fear is maturing also. Take for instance the average pregnant woman. As the signs of sharp pains get more frequent and intense, she knows she is drawing very close to the stage of child birth.

What signs reveal the starting point of fear?

What signs reveal a maturing process that is going on?

What signs reveal a fully matured or grown fear?

The signs are so important because it keeps a wise man on guard. May God give us wisdom to be on guard as He reveals these things to us in Jesus name.

SIGNS AND STAGES

The earliest sign is a desire to disobey God.

King Saul's disobedience were all based on fear. And it kept on until there was no deliverance for him from it any more. His fears kept prompting him into deeper levels of disobedience.

Isaiah 57:11

"And of whom have you been afraid, or feared, That you have lied And not remembered Me, Nor taken it to your heart? Is it not because I have held My peace from of old That you do not fear Me?"

Whenever that inner drive to disobey God comes, know that fear is working undercover.

I Samuel 13:8 – 12, and 15:24 shows us king Saul's fears and how he disobeyed because of them.

What about Eve's approach. She was made to see herself as inadequate and not up to standard, and so, to meet up, she had to disobey.

This sign does not just operate out of nowhere, it is basically premised upon the priority we place on the person or people we obey at the expense of God.

That person or persons could be ideologies, philosophies, literature and systems.

There has never been a sitting on the fence in life. It is either you are here or there. You cannot be nowhere at all. Negative or positive. So, that desire to disobey God comes out of a heart that is already settled for someone else to be of higher priority than God Himself.

When you look at the life of king Ahab in the book of I Kings, one striking thing about him was a little hidden regard for God in his life.

Instances: I Kings 21:27 – 29

Here, he had just been rebuked and judged by God for evil conspiracy against Naboth, the Jezreelite. Ahab immediately humbled himself.

In I Kings 19:1, after he experienced the power of God at the "fire must fall contest" of Elijah against the evil prophets in the land, and how Elijah prayed and prevailed against the other prophets, Ahab got home that day with excitement to tell Jezebel all that had transpired in Israel.

Yet with all these Ahab was attributed as a wicked and evil king by scriptures. Why?

He prioritized obeying his wife Jezebel above obeying God.

I Kings 21:25 says

"But there was no one like Ahab who sold himself to do wickedness in the sight of the LORD, because Jezebel his wife stirred him up."

This could only mean that Ahab probably always disobeyed God because of his wife whom he feared above God. Your decision to disobey God at every point in time reveals a fear that is hidden, waiting to be born. It was hidden in King Saul and it kept growing until Saul became fully matured in fear.

The first sign is a desire to disobey God. This, I call the silent stage.

At this stage, it is difficult to tell that fear is around.

When you notice a desire to disobey God, know that there is something or someone you fear that you want to please. It could be a man of God, yourself, entertainment, friends or family.

PRAY

• Father give me a heart that puts You above all priorities in my life in Jesus name.

•   Father, give me a new approach to life that considers you above all else in Jesus name.

•   Every desire in me to disobey God I curse you in Jesus name. Die.

INSTANCES

In Ezra 5:1 to 6:1 – 15, after God, through the prophets Haggai and Zechariah, commanded the people to go on with the building of the temple the people started to work without caring about any permission from the king because God had spoken, and they feared God.

So, when oppositions against the construction arose in Ezra 5:3 – 5, the people did not stop the work because they will rather obey God than man, and because they were afraid of God and not the king. So, even when a report was being filed against them to king Darius, they still continued the construction work. Not afraid, fearing only God who told them to work.

Truth is, we disobey God primarily out of a silent fear in our hearts. Check yourself and be truthful to yourself, you will notice it is hidden there.

If fear is the opposite of faith and Hebrews 11:6 says:

"But without faith it is impossible to please Him, for he who comes to God must believe that He is, and that He is a rewarder of those who diligently seek Him."

Then, **without fear it is possible to please God.**

Let me rephrase it this way:

"But without fear it is possible to obey God because he who comes to God believes that He is, and that He is a rewarder of those who diligently seek Him."

Put fear to death and you will easily obey God. Eve feared she was not good enough and so wanted to measure up by disobeying. She did not receive what God had said about her. Genesis 1:26 – 28.

The same thing she tried attaining was what God had already told her she was.

Psalm 8:4 – 5

Verse 5. "For You have made him a little lower than Elohim, and have…"

Elohim here is God Himself. We humans were made like God Himself, just a little lower than Him. Not lower than angels as some think but a little lower than God. Besides Psalm 82:6 and John 10:34 – 35 tells us we are gods.

What Eve felt she was not and wanted to attain out of fear, she actually had but lost it in her fear.

Another instance that proves a desire to disobey God as a result of fear is found in Acts 4:19 (NIV)

"But Peter and John replied, 'judge for yourselves whether it is right in God's sight to obey you rather than God.' "

Peter and John were before the power players of the time. The same people that initiated and executed the plot to eliminate Jesus Christ, yet Peter and John were not afraid of these people. Peter and John kept on preaching at every opportunity.

If Peter and John had been afraid of these people, they would have disobeyed the task of preaching.

A third account of this is found in Exodus 3:1 – 10, After God spoke to Moses and told him that he will be the one to go to Pharaoh, and to bring the Hebrews out of Egypt the land of bondage, Moses responded in fear.

"...who am I that I should go to Pharaoh, and that I should bring the children of Israel out of Egypt?"

Moses was afraid and was willing to disobey God. This disobedience was born out of his fear of Pharaoh.

Also in Exodus 4:1 "Then Moses answered and said, 'but suppose they will not believe me or listen to my voice; suppose they say, 'The LORD has not appeared to you.' "

Another fear Moses nursed that made him unwilling to obey the divine order was the fear of rejection from his own people.

The desire to disobey God, or the thought of it is the starting point or sign that proves the presence of fear.

ANOTHER STAGE REVEALING FEAR: LOSS OF IDENTITY

A second stage that reveals fear is the loss of identity. At this stage, the victim is unwilling to try again. He is weighed down by self-pity.

This was the stage Moses was wallowing in while tending the flocks of his father in law Jethro.

At age forty Moses prepared himself to deliver Israel from Egyptian captivity. He made an attempt in that respect and failed, so he fled. See Acts 7:22 – 30

Moses initially believed in his God assigned purpose as verse 25 shows, but when the first attempt came with rejection and threats against his life by his own people, Moses gave up on himself, his destiny and God. Acts 7:25

"For he supposed that his brethren would have understood that God would deliver them by his hand, but they did not understand."

Moses was just very certain without any iota of doubt that his destiny was to deliver Israel from Egypt and he expected all his people in captivity to accept him, love him and rally to him. Unfortunately the opposite was the case.

Failure was staring sternly at Moses and he gave up. After giving up, he retired to desert life. He went into cattle breeding or animal husbandry because he was afraid. He gave up on ever trying. For forty more years, Moses could not make another attempt to achieve his vision. He made no move to actualize his dream anymore. He lost his God given identity.

Acts 7:30 "And when forty years had passed..."

He had made an attempt forty years ago, and when unsuccessful, he reclined at that position, not ready to go on.

At this stage Moses lost his identity.

What was his identity?

The identity God put in him that he had realized forty years ago was that of a deliverer. Acts 7:25

Moses' identity was that he was raised by God as a deliverer. To deliver every single Israelite from the hand of the Egyptians, Pharaoh and the Egyptian gods. This was an identity Moses had within himself that he once believed. Exodus 4:10,13.

But all these changed along the years in Moses' heart, so he began to see himself as not good enough, he relegated himself to live the life of sheep chasing. Why? He started redefining himself as against what God had impressed on his heart that he ought to be: a deliverer.

When you lose identity, that is, when you do not even want to try again in that positive, Godly course that you had failed in before, know for certain you are been buffeted by fear. This is one of the dynamics or workings of fear.

See also Elijah in I Kings 19:4 "...And he prayed that he might die, and said, 'it is enough! Now, LORD, take my life, for I am no better than my fathers!'"

What could make this mighty "fire speaking and fire commanding" prophet of God say he was not good enough and that he wanted to die?

A loss of identity was behind it all. The evil report from Jezebel in I Kings 19:2 had a demonic attachment to it. The spirit that causes a man to lose his identity was behind it.

PRAY

• God of heaven and earth, deliver me permanently today from every identity killing spirit in Jesus name.

- I refuse to lose my identity, I decree, I shall not lose my identity in Christ in Jesus name.

- Every lost identity in my life, by the blood of Jesus Christ, be fully restored now in Jesus name.

- O Lord, bring me to the knowledge of my identity in the name of Jesus.

- Give me understanding of my identity Lord Jesus in Jesus name.

- I reclaim my lost identity by the blood of Jesus Christ, in Jesus name.

The same Elijah that boldly confronted the prophets of Baal and destroyed all of them. That same Elijah that single handedly confronted the whole nation is now afraid.

Yes, this same Elijah lost sight of his identity and was not interested in trying again. So he had to be replaced by God. I Kings 19:15 – 17.

This stage of loss of identity is really dangerous, this is that stage that made Eve believe every word the serpent told her despite what God told her. She lost sight of her identity as one created in the image of God. She completely forgot who she was, and the fear at this stage completely overwhelmed her until there was no escape again for her.

"See a man fully aware of his divine identity, little, or nothing can move such a man."

If Elijah had not lost sight of his identity he would not have been moved by an empty threat from that witch of a queen called Jezebel.

Compare all these happenings to the time that the same Elijah was confronted by three different groups of soldiers. Elijah wasted two groups out of the three groups of battalions because as of then his identity had returned back. He was now conscious of his identity. Though by now he had been replaced. Too bad.

Ten spies out of the twelve Moses had sent were already at this level of fear. This was why they gave the report that they were like grasshoppers who will not be able to face the giants. Immediately these men set their eyes on those giants they made up their minds to disobey God and this made them loose their identities. Compare them to another man who was committed to obey God.

Joshua 14:6-12. A man that had his identity intact.

After forty years of asylum God had to work on Moses before Moses regained his identity, but Caleb never lost his identity, even after forty five years of waiting.

Joshua 14:10 – 11.

"And now, behold, the LORD has kept me alive, as He said, these forty five years, ever since the LORD spoke this word to Moses while Israel wondered in the wilderness; and now, here I am this day, eighty five years old."

"As yet I am as strong this day as on the day that Moses sent me; just as my strength was then, so now is my strength for war, both for going out and for coming in."

What a demonstration of confidence!

Though back then they failed because ten of them gave negative reports to the people, Caleb did not give up trying because he knew his identity. This stage demands that you watch carefully those who try to define you. Never let anyone define you wrongly.

Many today are afraid of standing for the truth because of some unreasonable ideologies and philosophies.

PRAY

• By the blood of Jesus I renounce any demonic operation trying to take away or change my God given identity, in Jesus name.

ANOTHER STAGE OF FEAR: HATE

In the book of I John, there is so much that God reveals concerning fear and how it relates to hate. Hate, from this book of scripture is a sign of fear. You may want to say you disagree with this, but understand what

I John 4:18-20 is saying.

"There is no fear in love; but perfect love casts out fear, because fear involves torment. But he who fears has not been made perfect in love."

"We love Him because He first loved us."

"If someone says, 'I love God ', and hates his brother, he is a liar; for he who does not love his brother whom he has seen, how can he love God whom he has not seen?"

Let me paraphrase these verses this way, from the angle of fear that we are discussing on.

I John 4:18 – 20 Paraphrased

Verse 18. "There is fear in hate (*because hate is the opposite of love*); and perfect hate casts in fear, because fear involves torment. (*If you have ever hated you will agree with me that it only brings torment to you.*) **And he who fears has not been made perfect in love.** (*Not made perfect in love because the opposite of love: hate, is still in that person.*)"

The bold and italicized sentence can therefore read like this: "...**And he who fears has being made perfect in hate.**"

Verse 19. ...

Verse 20. "If someone says, 'I love God', and hates his brother, he is a liar; (*the reason is that a thing can never be the source of two clearly opposite things. Example; hot and cold water from the same source. Remember James 3:10-12*)..."

We can never love if we hate, and we cannot hate when love is at work in us, and when love is at work, then fear is cast out but when hate, which is the opposite of love, is in us, know for certain that that is a sign that there is fear. It brings in fear.

See James 3:10 – 12 "Out of the same mouth proceed blessing and cursing. My brethren, these things ought not to be so."

"Does a spring send forth fresh water and bitter from the same opening?"

"Can a fig tree, my brethren, bear olives, or a grapevine bear figs? Thus no spring yields both salt water and fresh."

Take it or leave it. Believe it or not. Accept it or reject this truth that the Holy Spirit is revealing from the word of God.

If "Perfect love casts out fear," then, "hate/perfect hate casts in fear."

If you cannot afford love, you will never cast away fear. But when your currency in the heart is huge enough to contain love, fear is cast out completely.

Let's see instances:

- Genesis 37:3 – 8

Because of the prospects in the future of young Joseph his brothers hated him. Do you think it was just a hate out of jealousy? No o!

See what Genesis 37:20 reveals about this truth: "Come therefore, let us now kill and cast him into some pit; and we shall say, 'some wild beasts has devoured him.' We shall see what will become of his dreams!"

They were afraid of the future greatness of Joseph; the possibilities of Joseph, a small boy, their younger one ruling over them. They never wanted that, and so they nursed hatred, instead of taking note of their hate as a sign of fear and dealing with it, they nursed it. Their fear still came to pass many years later, during the great famine in Genesis 42:1 – 9.

As Job said in Job 3:25, "For the thing I greatly feared has come upon me..."

Whether you decide to swallow this pill or not, hate has a silent or hidden fear behind it that you have not come to terms with yet. Check properly, you will discover that fear is behind that hatred.

- Another instance is Jesus and the Jewish leaders of His day.

John 15:23 – 25

One major reason they all hated Jesus was that they were afraid of Him. He was taking all the glory, and all men were coming to Him. It was more than just jealousy, their hate manifested as jealousy, but behind it all was fear manifesting as hate. They craved all the accolades being showered on Jesus by the people but none was given to them so long as Jesus remained on the scene. They wanted it badly. John 11:46 – 48

Verse 48 "If we let Him alone like this, everyone will believe in Him, and the Romans will come and take both our place and nation."

They were more afraid of losing their place (their office, authority and power) than anything else. All the hatred for Jesus was out of fear that He is becoming the voice that others listen to. Hear this, when you begin to hate anyone, check, it is not just a matter of jealousy, fear has crept in and is silently working behind the scenes in your heart.

Joseph's brothers all knew how their father, Jacob, took the blessings and the place of Esau his elder brother. After all, they all experienced how their dad acted when it was time for him to meet Esau. He surely must have narrated to them the reasons for his fear of Esau. Having seen all these, it would be foolishness according to their own thoughts to permit a repeat in their own time.

So, by their wisdom, the only way to stop such a repeat of that which they greatly feared (their younger brother ruling them) was to hate and eliminate the young Joseph. After all, his dreams were showing the likelihood of him collecting the blessings of the first son. This was the fear that led to hatred. The hatred was only a sign revealing their fear.

• Another example to consider is that of King Saul and the young, wise and energetic David.

I Samuel 18:5 – 9

David, an innocent young man returning from war was welcomed with songs and praises from the women. Little did he envisage that they were digging a deep grave of hatred for him in the mind of King Saul. Saul began hating David from that day because David was getting too popular. It was not just a matter to be seen facially as jealousy. King Saul feared that the throne will be given to David and he, the king, may become a no body. His hatred for David was a sign pointing to the existence of fear in his heart. Reading through the last pages of I Samuel, Jonathan, King Saul's son, had a different approach. He had no fear of David becoming king. No fear of becoming a no body. So Jonathan loved David as himself. I Samuel 18:1 – 3 and 20:17.

See it in this light.

What I fear I will certainly hate. The reason is that such gives me heartaches, and it troubles me.

If I fear rats, certainly I will hate rats. And if I am not afraid of a thing I cannot hate it. This goes on to say that the moment we fear sin because of what we know it can do to us, we will begin to hate it at all cost.

See Hebrews 1:9 "You have loved righteousness and hated lawlessness; Therefore God, Your God, has anointed You with the oil of gladness more than Your companions."

The fear of what sin does to us should put a hatred in our hearts for sin.

See Matthew 26:39, 42. Jesus, out of fear of what sin can do, desired that the burden of being forsaken by God should pass away from Him. Yet because of love in His heart, He permitted it to be so, also because it was the Father's will. Matthew 27:46

"...My God, My God, why have You forsaken Me?" The sins of the whole world He was carrying on the cross was why God forsook Him at that point. God's eyes are too pure they cannot behold iniquity.

This also is the heart we are expected to have in dealing with the sin issue. A heart of fear for the losses sin can cause us, and this fear gives birth to total hatred for sin. The hatred helps us avoid it.

PRAY

• Lord, put the hatred for sin and every ungodliness in my heart, in Jesus name.

• Father, cause me to hate sin with perfect hatred in Jesus name.

• Lord, cause me to be conscious of the losses that sin brings so I can always flee from every sin.

ANOTHER STAGE OF FEAR: IMPATIENCE

Impatience: being annoyed or irritated by somebody or something especially because you have waited for a long time.

Another subtle sign that fear is working is when impatience is seen in a life. A hurry to get that thing might not necessarily be out of diligence or commitment, but out of impatience.

See this in I Samuel 13:5 – 13, verses 11 – 12

"And Samuel said, 'what have you done?' Saul said, 'When I saw that the people were scattered from me, and that you did not come within the days appointed, and that the Philistines gathered together at Michmash,

then I said, 'The Philistines will now come down on me at Gilgal, and I have not made supplication to the LORD.' Therefore I felt compelled, and offered a burnt offering.'"

King Saul waited for seven days as revealed in I Samuel 13:8, but along the line, out of fear he did what was not in his jurisdiction to do. That fear revealed itself through impatience. He had already waited seven days, just a few hours or minutes before the arrival of Samuel, and then he got restless and impatient and went on to offer the sacrifice.

Many times in our lives when life pushes us against the walls, we run out of gas and impatience causes us to take some steps because we were afraid. We cannot wait anymore. We have tried our best in waiting this long. We have done all we think is expected of us. Why no results.

The impatience that is pushing us to act amiss only reveals that we are afraid. Fear is really a killer. It is the cause of most problems in the world today. No wonder God in several places in the scripture always commands

His people to "Fear not." In fact, bible scholars tells us there are about 365 'FEAR NOT' in the bible. If this is anything to go by, it means our major problem in life, apart from sin, is fear which in itself is a sin.

So, we have one "FEAR NOT" for each day of the year (365 days in a year.)

See James 1:2 – 4. "My brethren, count it all joy when you fall into various trials,"

"Knowing that the testing of your faith produces patience."

"But let patience have its perfect work, that you may be perfect and complete, lacking nothing."

This is saying, in effect, that the proving of faith gives patience. Now fear is the opposite of faith, so if the trying of our faith births patience, therefore, where

there is no faith to try or prove, the opposite (fear) will be the only available thing to test or prove. The opposite of what the proving of faith produces will be the only thing that will be produced. This opposite is nothing but impatience.

So verse 3, paraphrased, could read something like this:

"Knowing that the testing of your lack of faith (fear) produces impatience."

Remember the perfection that comes out of love which is the opposite of hate according to I John 4:18, also verse 4 of James 1 shows us that there also is a perfection that is born out of patience, and this patience comes by the testing of our faith. These two, put side by side proves that:

Love (opposite of hate) = perfection

Patience (opposite of impatience) = perfection

Therefore

Since fear births hate

And fear births lack of faith,

Then lack of faith is the mother of impatience, a sign of the presence of fear.

In many parts of the world today, a lot of unmarried people (more ladies tend to fall victim) have entered into marriages that became a night mare for them because of impatience. This happens because they feel they have waited long enough. This impatience is primarily born out of a silent fear that they have nursed. Fear that as ladies time is no longer on their side

I personally have lost things in life due to impatience. This was born out of a bid to get some things done in a hurry. This was because I was afraid of some things, time being part of my fears.

Impatience is one reason we hardly want to wait for God to move before we make our moves. This impatience is due to fears after a long or brief wait.

Fear is so subtle, and it is a killer. We hardly notice it is there. We talk about the surface issues many times when the real root is fear.

As you very well know, fear steals your peace, and that is why impatience kills peace. This lack of peace of mind keeps dragging you to act quickly until you have taken the action hastily only to be full of regrets later.

May God help us to stand firm in Jesus name. Amen.

ANOTHER STAGE OF FEAR: MEANING ATTACHED TO THINGS

Amos 3:6a says "If a trumpet is blown in a city, will not the people be afraid?"

Day to day life experiences have caused so many of us to attach meanings to some particular things. When such attached meanings are born out of past negative experiences, even if the thing in itself does not really mean any negative thing, then it becomes a noticeable sign of fear in that life.

In Genesis 26:1 – 3, immediately the famine began, we see Isaac run to the Philistines, and was ruminating on crossing over to Egypt before God stopped him. Isaac, I believe, took this move and prepared to take the next one (to go to Egypt) because experience had taught him through Abraham's life to attach certain meanings to famine. To him famine is the time to run to Egypt the only place to survive during a famine. God had to prove this idea wrong to him as he later obeyed God and stayed back in the land of the Philistines.

Dr. Mike Murdock in his message on: THE SEVEN POWERS OF THE MIND narrated a story I will like to share.

> To test the power of the mind, researchers took a football team into a special room. And a doctor told all of
>
> them after a series of medical examinations that they all had a bacteria. A disease discovered in their physical examination. And that they'll be observed over time. In seven days, two of the football players could not get out of bed. Every one of them developed symptoms. One, his legs were hurting so painfully, another the back, and some others all kinds of problems evolved after the doctors report that they had discovered some disease in the body of these footballers.
>
> After two weeks, every single one of the footballers had something wrong

seriously. They were aware there were symptoms. Then the doctors had to tell them there was really nothing wrong with them that they were only testing the POWER OF SUGGESTIONS. How that the mind can take a thought and turn it into an experience.

What a test!

These footballers, when told of the disease (suggestion) began to attach a meaning to it and that became fear, and that fear gave birth to chemical and demonic reactions and activities that brought physical

manifestations of what such disease (suggestion) could cause. You see, immediately we attach a meaning to anything, the physical manifestation of that thing begins to come to bare.

Look at Amos 3:6a again.

The reason the people will be afraid when the trumpet is blown is because there is a pre-attached meaning to the sound of the trumpet. This pre-attached meaning is why even when something had not even really happened, the presence of another thing will cause or raise panic/fear in anticipation of the manifestations of the meaning attached. Understanding of this is handy in dealing with ailments that try to attack our bodies.

The footballers quickly defined the proposed or suggested disease and its symptoms and began to fear it. And before you knew what was happening, the definition yielded negative results in their lives. This is food for thought.

FEAR AT ITS PEAK: WITHDRAWAL

See Adam and Eve's story in Genesis 3:8 – 10. These individuals that once walked boldly and freely in the garden suddenly began to hide. They withdrew due to fear. Self-pity works very much at this stage. Study a person that withdraws from others (not withdrawal

based on trying to keep away from mixing with wrong characters). It majorly comes out of fear. When you notice a once joyful and easy going child suddenly withdrawn, watch it, you can be certain something must have happened to the child that he or she is afraid to talk about; psychologists will tell you

FEAR AT ITS PEAK: SUICIDE

Judges 16:26 – 30

An ex-champion now turned a miller in the mills of the Philistines. A one time champion now without eyes, caused by the hand of a woman.

Samson thought on all these and more, to a point he feared his reproach, defeat, and shame. So, the only way was suicide. I tell you, it will take a lot of faith to be in these shoes that Samson walked into and not contemplate what he also did. But one can, with the grace of God decide not to end this way. God is able to deliver anyone; for with God, nothing shall be impossible.

How do I face my family?

How do I live among people this way, without eyes?

His former status and reputation all came staring at his face.

Check most people that have attempted suicide, there was a silent fear that drove them to such dangerous points. The point of attempting to take their own lives.

PRAY

• Father, have mercy on me and deliver me totally from my fears in Jesus name.

CHAPTER 5

TROPHIES OUTSIDE FEAR

There are so much benefits to be maximized and enjoyed where fear is absent. A lot has being revealed within the confluence of fear, and so far, I believe no right thinking individual will in anyway desire any of its workings. Every reasonable human being wants peace, love, acceptance and all the qualities that make for a proper life. These and more are only possible outside fear as discussed. The reason is that when fear operates, these things become a mirage.

So, the desirable life or trophies exists only outside of this fear. What are these trophies?

I Samuel 21:8 – 9

In these verses, David demanded for something and he got the trophy, a prize. Remember how David had to fearlessly put his life on the line to bring down Goliath when others fled. David dealt with that fear and the trophy or victory he secured through God became his testimony that brought him more victories in the remaining days of his life.

Hear David's testimony about that Sword: "...There is none like it; give it to me"

Imagine the whole picture.

118

David, a young lad faced a giant warrior, Goliath, and fearlessly knocked him down by the help of God. He then climbs on the giant and pulls out the giant's sword from him. The next thing we see is David chops off the head of the giant with the sword. Many years later, David was again with that same sword from the giant, with this sword he faced many other enemies in his life.

The example shows that, whenever David went to any battle and held that sword, no matter the enemy that he faced, he will simply look at that sword which originally belonged to the giant. As he looks, God gets his attention, and all of a sudden the whole scenario of how he was able to be a giant slayer will rush back to his mind. There and then, David will recall: "it was because I involved God in that battle that I got this trophy (goliath's sword)." Whenever this occurs, David runs back to God in his heart as he fights.

When he feels tired at the battle front, just a look at the sword in his hands reminds him: "if Goliath couldn't kill me, then these present enemies cannot."

It takes only you, to possess your trophy despite the fears of today to give you mouthwatering victories tomorrow. You and I must, like David, seize our trophies despite fear and face all our giants in life.

Growing up as a young convert, I realized that I had severe stomach aches whenever I embark on a dry fast. (Fasting without food for days, sometimes taking only water). In trying to understand if this was the normal thing with everyone who embarks on a dry fast, I started to observe anyone who was on such a fast. But to my amazement, none of the elderly or younger people I observed had any of this sign. So I started asking direct questions from people concerning it, and no one I knew had this issue. This aches were so terrible that during such fasts I shut myself indoors away from people to manage the agony. Strange it seems yet painful, but I never gave up on such fasts.

This pains were not hunger pangs, do not misinterpret that. At such times, in order to give myself some relief, I decided not to swallow saliva in my mouth because it aggravates the situation. So I spit out frequently. The frequent spitting happens to be one of the reasons I lock myself away from people then whenever I embark on such fasts. All this discomfort did not deter me. I always prepare my mind for the agony I will face when I want to embark on such a fast.

When I asked people around how I should deal with this challenge, my goliath, many suggestions were proffered but none worked. Until one night during a prayer session via phone with my friend while on a dry fast. As the aches were getting severe I quickly requested her to please permit me to get a little relief as the pain was really excruciating. She enquired what it was and I explained to her my age long ordeal. We ended the call and I tried lying with my belly on the floor to get some relief.

To the glory of God as soon as we ended the call, she kept interceding on my behalf, unknown to me. And to my surprise when I woke up in the morning, the pains were completely gone. There was no single sign of pain. I was amazed. I called her that morning and she told me of the supernatural experience she had while she was praying for me concerning the stomach. I have been completely healed since then.

The truth is that if I had stopped going on dry fasts due to those pains, I would never have received that "trophy" that night. I refused to fear the pains and excruciating aches and I have my trophy in this regard. Today I can embark on a dry fast and not be moved. Hallelujah.

Trample on your fear from its very source, anywhere it tries to show itself the most. Shut it down right there.

You and I must decide to throw fear to the ground and beat it so mercilessly. It will not ever want to take us for a ride again. Throw fear to hell because that is where it belongs. It was not meant for our hearts. It is not for us. It is until we do this that we receive our trophy (the testimony) that we look at and remind ourselves of what Jesus has done for us. This helps us to press on for more.

Revelations 12:11 says "And they overcame him by the blood of the Lamb and by the word of their testimony, and they did not love their lives to the death."

Conquer that fear and receive a trophy that will be a testimony you can use for another issue or challenge in years ahead; so you can give a shout that God who gave you the victory of yesterday will give you that of today.

These are trophies outside of fear to provide courage for more testimonies.

See Ruth's case in Ruth 1:7 – 8

Ruth was faced with all the fears and uncertainties of leaving her native land to go to Judah with Naomi her mother-in-law. All the realities of the uncertainties were before her yet these realities created no iota of fear in Ruth that could defeat her. Her mind was made up.

She damned the consequences because of the God of Israel. Her first testimony was finding favor before Boaz in whose field she gleaned. This trophy helped her to look up with high hopes for a better tomorrow in coming years in Judah. Finally, we see her marry Boaz, and later she became a foremother of Jesus Christ through the lineage of King David.

When you decide to stay outside of fear, you cannot imagine the trophies, or testimonies that awaits you.

The bible is full of several examples of those who stayed outside fear: Caleb, Joshua, Apostle Paul, Jesus Christ Himself etc. Hebrews 12:1 – 2.

See the personalities in the Faith Hall of Fame as revealed in Hebrews 11:1 – 40.

As you now know, faith is the direct opposite of fear. What I am driving at therefore is that your dwelling should be with Faith, not fear. It is in faith that you can acquire these trophies. Faith is more than just boldness, it is believing "God can do this for me, God can handle it".

Faith is not about you, but knowing that with God all things are possible. That is when the trophy is won. Was it just boldness that gave David the head of Goliath? No, it was more than that. Faith did it. The "God can kill this uncircumcised Philistine" attitude.

Outside of fear, is a track record of possibilities that keeps driving you to lay hold on more. It is not you. I will usually say; "I've seen God do crazy things." Crazy here, I mean abnormal things. Things that are normally beyond the realm of possibilities.

When you are in a bus, the dynamics of that bus affects you, but when you step out of the bus and get into an airplane you are released from the dynamics of a bus and made to experience the dynamics of an airplane. This is what is tenable in regard to the subject.

Fear breeds failure in people, and finally kills them. That is part of its dynamics. Failures receive no trophy in a competition, only winners or champions do. And champions are found outside fear because that is where their trophies are located.

After God dealt with Moses' fear at the burning bush encounter, his rod (ordinary shepherd's rod) became a focal point of the move of God in his generation. Moses' confidence, I believe, got renewed whenever he held that rod, and he recalls everything God had done through the rod. This encourages him to press on.

II Kings 2:12 – 15

Elisha fearlessly followed the same man (Elijah) that Jezebel sought to kill; not afraid for his own safety. Finally he got the trophy, the mantle of Elijah. This trophy gave him a sense of confidence and boldness that geared him to knock down and knock out situations. Trophies are very important because they give you a sense or hope of what can still be done or achieved. And that is why you must get them. Look outside that fear, you can locate a trophy.

PRAY

• Lord help me lay hold of all my trophies outside fear in Jesus name.

CHAPTER 6

FREEDOM FROM FEAR

I presume that nobody in life hates freedom. That is why nations fight for independence. This is also the reason for many revolutions and counter revolutions worldwide. A people get to a point in their existence that they are totally fed up with the patterns they consistently see in their lives. Either patterns created by their leaders or by their own consistent foolishness and errors. This begins the breaking point for such a people, and at this stage, all they begin to canvass for is freedom at any cost. Change from the status quo no matter the price.

Everyone wants to be free. It is in the human DNA. Though freedom comes with a lot of responsibilities. There are limits to what we can and should do when we are free. In the sphere of things in the human system, God has given us freedom, yet that freedom has boundaries that guide it. See Galatians 5:13, James 1:25, James 2:12, I Peter 2:16

So we are encouraged to look into the perfect law of liberty, yet not to forget the restrictions in it, and to remember that we will be judged by that same law of liberty. Freedom is good, but we must decide to live within its limits, else no other sacrifice can be offered for us. Hebrews 10:26

PRAY

•   Lord Jesus, please cause me never to enter into any willful sin again till I see you in glory in Jesus name.

Besides, when a person is caged or held in prison by someone, it will take some measure for the prisoner before he can come out.

Acts 16:25 – 26, 38 – 40

Until the prison doors are opened, only then is one freed from prison.

In Exodus 12:29 – 33, when God opened up the doors of the prisons that shut the Israelites in Egypt, the Israelites received their freedom and went out of the land of Egypt. Their freedom came as a result of the opening of their prison doors. Acts 12:1 – 10.

In Joseph's case, Genesis 41:14, a higher authority ordered the prison keepers to bring him out and free him. An order or decree got him out of prison.

Whatever the case, freedom comes by authority.

Like a prison, fear is a very terrible and wicked spirit that seeks to steal, kill and destroy its victims.

John 10:10

As Isaiah 14:17 puts it, fear does not set its prisoners free. There is no official prison term with fear. Victims must remain in it till they die. Fearful people are serving a perpetual prison term; a life sentence except they make effort to break loose.

But there is hope. Hope through the highest authority in the whole universe, Jesus Christ. Isaiah 49:22, 24 – 26 says God shall lift His hands and things will begin to take shape for that freedom to be absolutely and permanently effected. And it goes on to say that even if the jailers say it is their legal right to hold the captive, He, God, will contend with them, and save the captive.

Contend with them could mean

• If they take the matter to court, I will appear as an advocate and contend with them there.

• If they take it to the battle ground, I will take up a sword and a shield to contend with them.

"So, no matter where they take your case, to keep you in bondage, I will contend with them and set you free." That's God speaking.

Hear this: Isaiah 50:7 - 9

Verse 7. "For the Lord God will help me;..."

Verse 8. "He is near who justifies Me; who will contend with Me? Let us stand together. Who is my adversary? Let him come near Me."

Verse 9. "Surely the Lord God will help Me;"

Hear this, you need divine help to be free from fear. Fear is the weapon of Satan, our arch enemy. It takes God to help a man out of the devil's hands. In all the different cases we have considered in this volume, it is evident that only divine intervention can help a man out of fear.

No wonder Psalm 46:1 assures us that God is a very present help in trouble (in fear). To receive this help there must be a crying out to God.

Psalm 18:2 – 3, 6, 17

Verse 3. "I will call upon the LORD who is worthy to be praised; so shall I be saved from my enemies."

Verse 6. "In my distress I called upon the LORD, And cried out to my God; He heard my voice from His temple, And my cry came before Him, even to His ears."

Verse 17. "He delivered me from my strong enemy, From those who hated me, For they were too strong for me."

remember how God delivered me recently from the rage of fear that came all over me from nowhere. I had to raise my voice in holy anger to God against this fear and He delivered me. This fear came in the cause of this write up and it took many days before it got totally cleared out from my heart, and as I did not keep silent over it. I sensed Satan resisting this work by attacking me with the same subject severally. Glory be to God who always sets me free, and He can set you free too.

Anyone who will be delivered from fear must be willing to be delivered. Hear what David said:

Psalm 18:4, 6

"The pangs of death surrounded me, And the floods of ungodliness made me afraid."

"In my distress I called upon the LORD, And cried out to my God; He heard my voice from His temple, And my cry came before Him, even to His ears."

In the midst of king David's fears he cried out to God and was delivered.

In Matthew 14:25 – 30, there was a crying out for deliverance. You must be able to cry out if you must be freed from the prison of fear.

Fear is not just a state or condition of the mind, it is a spirit and that is why you must cry aloud.

In Exodus 14:15 – 16, when they sighted Pharaoh's invading army like a flood, the Israelites got scared, Moses cried out to God and deliverance came.

An illustration to buttress this truth is this: if rescue commandos are to be sent to rescue prisoners of war, or any category of prisoners, those prisoners must either be nationals of the nation sending forth the rescue team or citizens of an ally nation. This means that relationship matters. If it works this way in the natural realm, how much more in the spiritual? Spiritual laws are quite very strict. To get this help from God means God also must consider who you are. Your spiritual nationality or allegiance.

The good news is, even if you are in no way related to God *(the way to be related to a person indeed is by blood or adoption, so it also takes the blood line of Jesus Christ and adoption by the Holy Spirit to be related to God),* you can be. This then gives God legal ground to deal with every single issue of fear contending with you. II Timothy 1:7 reveals the portion of those related to God.

What I am trying to say is that you must surrender your life to Jesus Christ as your personal Lord and savior so that God can finish the fear you are combating with.

Without surrendering your life to Jesus, God will be seen as a law breaker.

TO SURRENDER YOUR LIFE TO JESUS CHRIST:

Romans 10:9 – 11

• **Believe in Jesus Christ as God's son manifest in the flesh**

• **Believe Jesus Christ died for your sins, was buried, and resurrected again**

• **Believe He can and will save you.**

• **You must humble yourself and forsake all contrary world views and philosophies and systems and beliefs**

• **You must confess Him with your mouth as Lord.**

If you are willing to accept Jesus Christ then take this prayer of confession.

LORD JESUS CHRIST, I CONFESS I AM A SINNER DESERVING JUDGEMENT. I BELIEVE YOU ARE THE SON OF GOD WHO DIED FOR ME. YOU WERE BURIED AND YOU RESURRECTED.

PLEASE COME INTO MY LIFE. SAVE ME FROM ALL MY SINS AND THE POWER OF SIN. I ACCEPT YOU INTO MY LIFE AS MY LORD AND PERSONAL SAVIOR FROM TODAY. WRITE MY NAME IN THE BOOK OF LIFE. REMOVE MY NAME FROM THE BOOK OF DEATH.

BAPTIZE ME WITH YOUR HOLY SPIRIT. THANK YOU JESUS FOR SAVING ME.

I DECLARE THAT I AM A CHILD OF GOD. I AM BORN AGAIN AND I WILL WALK WITH JESUS TILL THE END IN JESUS NAME.

If you have made this confessions then congratulations. One more thing, run away from sin. Look for a good bible (I recommend King James Version, New Living Translation or New King James Version) and read daily to build your spirit. Make sure you talk to God daily in Jesus' name. Also get a true bible believing church where sin is not tolerated and love with Godly fear is practiced and fellowship there. Make sure it's a church centered on Jesus' teachings. God bless you.

Now that you are free indeed. Cry out confidently now to God as a child of God.

PRAY

• **You spirit of fear operating in my life, I am no longer your candidate from today. I belong to Jesus in Jesus name.**

- I renounce you spirit of fear, I renounce every power of fear over me in Jesus name because it is written according to 1 Peter 2:9 "But you are a chosen generation, a royal priesthood, a holy nation, His own special people, that you may proclaim the praises of Him who called you out of darkness into His marvelous light."

- I am God's holy nation therefore I come out of every prison of fear now by the blood of Jesus Christ in Jesus name.

- I answer: "Yes Lord Jesus" to Your call out of darkness into God's marvelous light in Jesus name.

- Fear, let your darkness over me expire permanently now in Jesus name.

- Jesus Christ the son of God, please deliver me completely and permanently from all these fears (MENTION EACH OF THE FEARS YOU ARE EXPERIENCING) in Jesus name.

- Lord Jesus Christ, cause the light of Your countenance to shine on me and drive every spirit of fear permanently away to the pit of hell in Jesus name

- Hold my hands Lord Jesus Christ and Lead me all the way through from today till the end in Jesus name.

This is just the crying out stage of freedom from fear. There is the sustenance stage which helps to maintain this victory. This sustenance stage has to do with a series of a life time of discipline that will keep fear permanently away.

Know this, the sustenance stage is too important to be ignored.

Matthew 12:43 – 45. Please it is very important to do this frequently. An empty container under normal circumstances will continue to have air in it until someone fills it with something.

This stage requires the following: Romans 12:1 – 2

"I beseech you therefore, brethren, by the mercies of God, that you present your bodies a living sacrifice, holy, acceptable to God, which is your reasonable service."

"And do not be conformed to this world, but be transformed by the renewing of your mind, that you may

prove what is that good and acceptable and perfect will of God."

These points us to a way we must daily live to remain out of fear.

•   We must daily make our lives pleasing and appealing to God. That is, a pleasing sacrifice. This means it is going to cost you severely. The cost is that there are many things you want to do, but for Christ's sake and for your own good, you will rather not do. The purpose is for consistent holy living.

• You cannot accept, agree or even adapt to the systems of this evil world anymore. Luke 4:5 – 8. Satan rules the systems of this world and he masterminds fear. Accepting the world system by conforming to it is coming under Satan's rule.

• Mind transformation. This entails the kind of things you begin to permit into your mind. What a mind focuses on will soon become a strong hold in that mind. What you watch, and listen to and read must change for good. This goes on to include the type of friends you keep. They must be positive and upright people. I Peter 1:22. Study, read, meditate on the scriptures.

• II Corinthians 10:4 – 5. Consciously reject all thoughts that breed fear and stand against them with firmness in the word of God.

• You need to build a life of consistent prayer. You must learn to just pray and pray aggressively, Satan and his hosts are not gentlemen.

• Learn never to give up in the place of prayer. If it seems there is no answer, go back again and again, and again until you get it.

Let this word in Luke 1:73 – 75 guard our hearts daily:

"The oath which He swore to our father Abraham:"
"To grant us that we, Being delivered from the hand of our enemies, Might serve Him without fear,"
"In holiness and righteousness before Him all the days of our life."

God has sworn, and He is faithful. He has sworn to grant us to be delivered from the hands of our enemies, so we can serve Him without fear in holiness and righteousness all our lives. That is, when you request to be delivered from the enemies, your fears, God will grant that request and you in turn will certainly be delivered from their hands. And you must serve God in that new state of liberty.

There are many ways to serve God. Evangelism is the main service that God has called us all to do. Worship is the root of it all. But others can include: sweeping your local church, and cleaning the chairs there, or singing in the choir, or ushering, or visitation, or funding outreaches and projects etc.

Besides, as you go about your circular job or business, serve God in every capacity as you make Him known and display His power in your work and business place.

God is even more set to deliver us from fear than we think because He loves us and desires our worship and service without fear.

In concluding this chapter, listen to this beautiful testimony from one of my sisters in Christ, sister Ogbiloja Patience.

"She had previously discussed her fear with me after service one Sunday morning. This fear had deprived her of many things. I counseled her briefly and then prayed with her. To the glory of God, she informed me weeks later of the victory God had given her in regard to the fears. Hear the way she puts it in her own words: 'Yes sir. I have overcome the spirit of fear completely.'" (Shared by her permission)

This is awesome to hear and see, that a family member of the body of Christ is liberated from fear. This is God's will for us all so we can serve Him without fear.

She is an over-comer as the scripture states, "they overcame him by the blood of the Lamb and by the word of their testimony".

CHAPTER 7

THE FEAR OF GOD

Talking about an epidemic that's ravaging a people and saying nothing at all about a panacea is like adding salt or pepper to a wound on the body. What such a talk will end up achieving is breed more fear and panic that will eventually hasten the damage such epidemic will do to its victims. The fear and panic are enough death pills, apart from the epidemic itself. Just like the research on the power of suggestions shared earlier. If those footballers were told of a possible solution for the suggested disease, they would not have been struck down by fear so easily.

Having spoken much about fear and its solutions, we must talk about the fear of God because, as was pointed out in the previous chapter, there is no vacuum in nature. Even what the scientist calls space is full of countless meteors, stars, and other planetary bodies. Besides, when it relates to spiritual things, there is really no vacuum anywhere.

This calls for the wisdom in discussing the fear of God.

Matthew 12:43 – 45 and Luke 11:24 – 26 proves the necessity for this. When an unclean spirit (fear) leaves an abode, it goes out looking for another one and finds none. So it goes back to the one it left, and when he finds it clean and empty, he goes to invite seven more wicked spirits than itself to join him to reoccupy that space. So the last state of the victim becomes worse than the initial.

This calls for the exigency of talking about the "FEAR OF GOD". This is a very broad, and sensitive topic to discuss. The need for the fear of God cannot be overemphasized because that is the only true opposite of fear that can occupy the clean and well-arranged house. The fear of God is the only true occupant that can rightly face off the fear that was discussed earlier in the previous chapters.

From many scriptures, we see diverse meanings of the "Fear of God" and also how they were applied in several scenarios. The first mention of the fear of God in the bible can be traced in Genesis 20:8 – 11.

This was the case between Abraham and Abimelech king of Gerar when Abraham and Sarah mutually lied to Abimelech about Sarah's status as being Abraham's sister instead of wife.

One striking point is found in verse 11. "And Abraham said, 'Because I thought, surely the fear of God is not in this place; and they will kill me on account of my wife.'" So, what Abraham meant invariably was: "I thought there was no fear of God here, but I can now see that the fear of God is here." The fear of God in this first report and use of the term fear of God came in correlation with the display of an action or a disposition or character. Let us analyze it :

• Abimelech had a new woman added to the ones he had earlier.

• Abimelech was rebuked by God to be making a fatal error that is adultery.

• Abimelech quickly did restitution.

• Abimelech rebuked Abraham but never fought him.

We can see a heathen king display a rare virtue that is not common among nations.

What was Abraham's fears :

• They will kill me because of Sarah.

• They will take Sarah my wife forcefully.

These fears in his heart made him think there was no fear of God there.

In connecting these two we can check similar events in scripture to relate with.

I.   Genesis 34:1 – 3

Schechem a prince of Hivite descent took Dinah, Jacob's daughter, and forced himself on her. Yet in verse 19 of Genesis 34, we read the following: "So the young man did not delay to do the thing, because he delighted in Jacob's daughter. He was more honorable than all the household of his father."

How honorable?

Well I cannot say. Yet it brings a thought in my heart. Why should he force Dinah if he was honorable?

I assume, it is a lack of the fear of God. The word honorable here could mean one highly respected for whatsoever reasons. Compare him with Amnon in

II Samuel 13:6 – 7, 10 – 14

This act was what Abraham feared that made him succumb to a lie thereby denying Sarah as his wife. See this other case study. So, Abimelech will not do such because he had the fear of God.

II.   Genesis 39:7 – 10, 11 – 12.

Joseph had the gates of adultery widely opened for him to indulge in, yet he chose another way. He fled. Why? What differentiated him from Amnon and Schechem? The answer is not farfetched; it was the fear of God.

This was exactly what Abimelech, king of Gerar did immediately he discovered that Sarah was another man's wife. Abimelech fled for his life. He returned the man's wife to him and rebuked the man for exposing his nation to national sin and divine judgment.

From these scenarios we can establish that there is actually a standard measurement with which "the fear of God" is checked. That measurement scale is called the character of God. The integrity of God. That is the standard.

This is why in checking the fear of God on that scale, men who with a pure motive did things but later found the outcome to be negative did all to right the wrong, even though it was not with wrong intentions that they had done what they did. They right the wrong not minding the cost.

That is where Abimelech comes in. He was a man with genuine fear of God. In trying some of us for the fear of God, actions carried out with good intentions will be allowed to yield the wrong results and heaven will just be watching if we will correct that which turned out negative.

The fear of God is a measuring of the actions of a man side by side the actions and character of God; how God acts.

The second time the fear of God is mentioned in the scriptures is in Genesis 22:11 – 12. See this:

Verse 11. "But the Angel of the LORD called to him from heaven and said, 'Abraham, Abraham!' So he said 'Here I am.'"

Verse 12. "And He said, 'do not lay your hand on the lad, or do anything to him; for now I know that you fear God, since you have not withheld your son, your only son from me.'"

Verse 12 specifically says: "...for now I know..."
For now I know could mean the following:
- All these years I was not so sure
- All these years I was skeptical of your fear of God
- I never knew until now.

What happened now that changed God's declaration and made Him attribute the fear of God to Abraham. It was due to an action Abraham took.

This was the same Abraham that had waited for 25 years before Isaac was born to him. Isaac by now should be probably about 12 years of age, as of the time he was to be sacrificed. So Abraham should be around 112 years of age. The point is this, that after all these years of following God, it is just now that God is telling Abraham that; "I now know you fear Me."

What caused Abraham to be attributed with the fear of God is summarized as follows:

Total and immediate obedience to God's instructions.

Why did God use this test to check Abraham's obedience?

•   Genesis 12:1 – 6. Abraham gave incomplete obedience.

Instruction was leave your father's house and land and go. How did Abraham comply?

He left his land of nativity-   Good

He went to Canaan-   Good

But he took a relative along-   Bad

God gave Abraham a chance later to correct the error when he and Lot had to separate. Genesis 13:5 – 16.

But God was still not satisfied, He still needed immediate and total obedience, not halfhearted obedience

.

Genesis 15. God came and promised a son to Abraham, verse 2 – 5. Yet in the next chapter after the promise, through Sarah's advice Abraham waited only for a short while and yielded to Sarah. It took several years later for

God to help Abraham correct that half obedience through the same Sarah. Funny! Genesis 21:9 -14
God was just watching for complete obedience. Not partial obedience.

• Then came the opportunity again. The third time.

I guess Satan, as it is customary with him, must have accused Abraham before God in regard to the matter, so Abraham had to be examined.

> Satan: "the only reason Abraham remains faithful is because of the son, Isaac, that You gave him."

God needed to prove Satan wrong and commend Abraham.
This test was not just about the sacrificing of Isaac, it is more than that. A test to determine how complete Abraham had become in maturity with God. Obedience without compromise no matter who must be disregarded.

In giving a test on the fear of God, prompt and complete obedience to divine instructions is needed to certify a person as having the fear of God. This is the fear of God.

Learn from Abimelech.

While walking to church some days back, I observed a little child (should be 3 or 4 years of age) around a small refuse heap. The little boy stooped down and was defecating. Not up to a minute later, I saw the boy leap up from his position with serious tears and shout. I was just wondering what it was when I sighted a herdsman leading a cow along that path. Not too far from the heap. I also observed as the boy leaped up that his eyes were on the direction the herdsman and his cow were coming through.

On seeing this I marveled greatly and said within me: "fear is really dangerous." Recall the definition of the dynamics of fear.

"Dynamics of fear is the way the feelings that fear gives you make you behave and react to the corresponding issues or situations."

So, **"the fear of the LORD is actually the way your view of God make you behave and react to issues or situations."**

Please notice the words: "Your views", "Your esteem of God"

If you have been following all through from chapter 1, you would have discovered that fear is a major factor behind why people have made so many wrong decisions.

Fear is like a driver or pilot. Fear is a controller.

A movie character said: "Everything in life is controlled by fear."

This comment holds a lot of truth in it. The sooner we see this critically and approach it wisely for our good and for the good of fellow men, the better.

This is why the fear of God is critical. In fact the fear of God is so paramount because just as the other fear controls people and makes them behave in a particular way, so does the fear of God make us do things in particular ways. Hear what Joseph – a noble prince of Egypt – said in Genesis 42:17 – 20

Verse 18. "Then Joseph said to them the third day, 'Do this and live, for I fear God:'"

"For I fear God." After this comment, Joseph gave instructions to the men, and he went on to release some of them and held one of them in prison. See it this way. Joseph was in essence telling them: "I have held you all for three days in prison, but because I fear God, I will behave towards you differently concerning this matter."

So Joseph could not take vengeance because of the fear of God. His behavior was born out of the fear of God.
The fear of God is the driving force that makes us do things in ways that correspond to the character of God.

Just imagine if Amnon and Schechem had the fear of God, it would have helped them to behave and react to those issues and situations in a different way.

Hear this from my father in the Lord – Pastor Enoch Adejare Adeboye.
"Above all, the fear of the Lord which is the beginning of wisdom is the climax of spiritual maturity that brings an individual into irreversible glory."
(Pst. E.A Adeboye, OPEN HEAVENS DAILY DEVOTIONAL; Tuesday 6th February, 2018).

So true, "The fear of the Lord is the climax of spiritual maturity."
So true because as every wind of doctrine blows around the spiritually immature, the matured ones will always

stay rigid, firm and well rooted. Ephesians 4:14 – 15. Why?

The babies are still convinced by any doctrine due to the room in their lives for other fears that control them and push them to succumb. Those who are mature just have the fear of the Lord which keeps them behaving only on God's character.

This is why they are mature. Through proper use they exercise their senses to discern wrong and right.

I Corinthians 3:1 – 3 and I Peter 2:2

You cannot be a true matured Christian if the baby characters are still found in you. It is not about how long you have been in the church or the pastoral office you occupy but it is about spiritual maturity.

If the fear of God is so important, then it is the determining factor for maturity. That is, the full expression of God's character, how then does it relate with Faith since:

• Hebrews 11:6 "Without faith it is impossible to please the Lord"

• Habakkuk 2:4 "The Just – righteous – shall live by faith."

Romans 1:17

HOW THE FEAR OF GOD RELATES WITH FAITH

Look at Exodus 1:17 – 21. Pharaoh gave a command to the midwives, but the midwives, having a good understanding of the DYNAMICS OF FEAR decided which fear they will allow to drive them. Either the fear of Pharaoh, or the fear of God. And wisely, they chose to be piloted by the fear of God rather than the fear of Pharaoh.

Verse 17. "But the midwives feared God, and did not do as the king of Egypt commanded them, but saved the male children alive."

Verse 21. "And so it was, because the midwives feared God that He provided households for them."

It is a decision we all must make. Either you fear God in respect to that decision and the fear drives you to act in line with what God says, or you fear another and get driven by the workings of that fear.

This is where the fear of God and faith comes into a sweet harmonious relationship. A beautiful harmony.

Anyone claiming to have faith but does not fear God is only displaying contradictions and he deceives himself.

From Hebrews 11:23 – 29

• Verse 23. There were two kind of fears that Moses' parents faced: the fear of God and the fear of

Pharaoh. They chose the fear of God and kept the baby alive. When they made that choice they probably did not have any idea of how to handle the matter of how to keep hiding the child when he begins to grow. Yet they did it anyway. "When we get to that bridge, God whom we fear will cross us over." That decision, based on the fear of God produces faith. The fear of God gave them a will that drove them into faith. Faith without the fear of God is dead. Faith without the fear of God is the kind that gets tired of God when He seems to be delaying.

• Verse 24 – 27. It was the right choice of fear that Moses had after God helped him to overcome the initial fear at the burning bush. This was the fear that drove Moses to undermine the powers and wrath of king Pharaoh. Moses refused to fear the Egyptian ruler, but he rather feared God only and so he stopped being recognized as Pharaoh's daughter's son. He was not afraid of the reproach of being an Israelite in Egypt. He feared only God in regard to the matter. Therefore the wrong kind of fear could not stop his destiny. Verse 25. He was well acquainted with the abject poverty with which his fellow Israelites lived, in Egypt, due to their enslavement. Moses was not afraid of this poverty. If he had, he would have chosen Egypt's recognition and not

Israel (Goshen) recognition. He rather chose the fear of God.

Verse 27 clearly reveals how Moses did not fear the king's wrath, and that of the whole of Egypt put together, He only feared God. The God his mother had instructed him of in the past, during the period that she nursed him for Pharaoh's daughter. Exodus 2:1 – 10. He did not forget this God.

Little wonder the day God introduced Himself to him as the God of his fathers: Abraham, Isaac, and Jacob, Moses immediately hid his face out of fear for God.
Exodus 3:2 – 6. This display of fear for God was later associated with faith. Hebrews 11:24a, 11:27a
So, the fear of God is what gives birth to true faith in God.

Abraham also demonstrated his faith through the fear of God. Genesis 22:12
"And He said, 'Do not lay your hand on the lad, or do anything to him; for now I know that you fear God, since you have not withheld your son, your only son, from Me.'"

Also Hebrews 11:17 – 19 says:

Verse 17. "By faith Abraham, when he was tested, offered up Isaac, and he who received the promises offered up his only begotten son,"

Verse 18. "of whom it was said, 'In Isaac your seed shall be called,'"

Verse 19. "Concluding that God was able to raise him up, even from the dead, from which he also received him in a figurative sense."

Genesis made us know how the fear of God was the driving force behind the attempted sacrificing of Isaac to God, and Hebrews gave a clearer explanation of the whole issue on faith. So, the fear of God gave birth to faith and that motivated Abraham to obey God.

Our faith is indeed dead without the fear of God.

Do not forget that faith without works is dead, also remember that fear drives actions. So, faith without the fear of God is really empty.

- Verse 28 – 29.
Verse 28. "By faith he kept the Passover and the sprinkling of blood lest he who destroyed the firstborn should touch them."
What does this mean?

Moses' adherence to the instructions given by God was born out of fear for God so God will not permit the destroying angel to touch any Israelite. The fear of God propelled Moses into an action of faith here.

Exodus 12:1 – 13.

And according to verse 29, it was by faith that they crossed the red sea. They were overwhelmed by the thought of who God is by reason of the things He had done, to a point that they did not fear passing through a sea, which on its own should have scared them. Ever imagined walking through a sea? It takes something else to do that, it is not ordinary. It needs the fear of God and faith.

Hebrews 11:32 – 39

All those mentioned had the promises given them, yet they did not receive it but kept on till death. Why till death?

This was because they were not afraid of swords, stones, saws, prisons and mockery. They feared no king, or authority apart from God, and it was imputed to them all as faith.

The fear of God leads us to have faith as it makes us do nothing contrary to undermine the character of God.

However, other fears propel many people to take contrary actions that displease God.

When the fear of God is in any life, that life easily has faith in God even when the realities and happenings convey contrary expectations. With the fear of God, no matter how long we have held on, we still keep holding on because our attention is fixed on God.

The day mankind begins to fear God, this whole world will be a safer, more peaceful and beautiful place to live.

One reason for the scarcity of true faith today is majorly due to the undermining of the fear of God in our societies.

As we stated earlier, fear takes the attention of people. This is why the fear of God gives birth to faith. It sets our attention on God.

Just like the little boy I previously talked about, his fear was the cow. And so long as his attention was given to the presence of the cow he behaved and reacted the way he did. But take that cow away and his behavior and reaction will definitely change. That is the power of fear. So it is even with adults.

When God is the only one we fear, our attention remains on Him and faith becomes consistent and it will always be of a real substance in our lives. In fact in Hebrews 11:7 we are told that:

"**By faith Noah,** being divinely warned of things not yet seen, **moved with Godly fear,** prepared an ark for the saving of his household, by which he condemned the world and became heir of the righteousness which is according to faith."

Noah by faith built an ark, but it was the fear of God that moved him. The fear of God activated the action he took which was an action of faith.

Without faith it is impossible to please God. Without the fear of God it is impossible to focus on God talk more of even having faith in his abilities. We need to let God grow and increase His fear in us so we can really serve Him well.

Workings of The Fear of God

Mark 9:2 – 6

Peter and the Zebedee brothers experienced the glory of God. Our fear of God must be daily renewed.

Revelations 1:17 – 18 reveals how John the beloved who although had had several encounters with Christ, yet during this encounter, a fresh fear came upon him. Yesterday's oil is not sufficient for today.

Mark 9:2 – 6, the encounter John had there made him afraid, yet in another encounter as recorded in Revelations, he fell before the Lord out of a renewed fear of God that came upon him.

Terrified by the light of God, Saul fell in total surrender to God out of fear in Acts 9:1 – 6. No one is able to remain on their feet when the fear of God is present. The fear of God in a man scares hell away.
Job 1:6 – 10, 2:1 – 6.

From several scriptures, we see that the fear of God is partly a function of the glory of God. Instances are found in Isaiah 6:1 – 5
On seeing the glory of the LORD, something positive happened in Isaiah's life. The reality of the fear of God came upon him and was renewed in his life.

In Exodus 3:1 – 6
On this day of the burning bush, Moses caught the fear of the LORD afresh and his life changed. This experience was the turning point for Moses' destiny forever. Other fears suddenly gave way. This was when Moses began to challenge other fears.
Do not dare any fear if you refuse the fear of God in your life.

The reason is that those other fears will turn on you and destroy you faster because there's no backup for you.

In Hebrews 12:18 – 26 the scripture reveals the kind of dispensation we live in. It is more dangerous than that of the Mount Sinai dispensation. Verse 25 – 26.
On Mount Sinai, it was so terrifying that Moses was so afraid.
Do not tell me: "It's the era of grace and so we have liberty to live anyhow." It is not so.
This era demands a totality of the fear of the LORD. Check Exodus 20:20
"... so that you may not sin."
The era of faith which is also an era of grace rejects sin because it is the era of the fear of the LORD.
One very interesting depiction of the fear of God can be found in the later chapters of the book of Job. Job 38 – 40:2

It will do you a lot of good if you check these chapters.
Hear what Job had to say after he understood the imagery God was using. It was a revelation of His glory to Job. Job 40:3 – 5

Verse 3. "Then Job answered the LORD and said:"

Verse 4. "'Behold, I am vile; what shall I answer You? I lay my hand over my mouth."
Verse 5. "Once I have spoken, but I will not answer; yes, twice, but I will proceed no further.'"

Job was terrified. Also the fear of God was renewed in him. Though Job was declared to be one who feared God, yet by the time God re-introduced and revealed Himself, Job was afraid of God, so much so that he said: "I lay my hand over my mouth."
Even with his comment God still was not through with him, but continued further in Job 40:6 – 41.

Job finally concludes by saying: Job 42:5 - 6
"I have heard of You by the hearing of the ear, But now my eyes sees You. Therefore I abhor myself, And repent in dust and ashes."

This is the fear of the LORD. Job initially only heard reports about God that allowed a low level of fear in him, but the day God personally introduced Himself to Job in a strange way, Job's fear of God became real. It changed so much that the fear of God in him now had substance.

Hear what Moses had to say concerning this issue. Exodus 20:19 – 20

"Then they said to Moses, 'you speak with us, and we will hear; but let not God speak with us, lest we die.' And Moses said to the people, 'Do not fear, for God has come to test you, and that His fear may be before you, so that you may not sin.'"

The revealed glory of God brought the fear of God, and that was what God wanted.

But, just as we have the free will to accept or reject, even so many have and can experience this glory and yet choose not to fear God.

Majority of the Israelites, during their exodus through the wilderness decided not to fear God, not minding all the miracles and revealed glories that they saw in their journey to Canaan. Only Joshua and Caleb made the choice to fear God.

Another example of this matter is Lucifer. Isaiah 14:12 – 17.

Verse 14. "I will ascend above the heights of the clouds, I will be like the Most High."

Why did he want this? The heights, and to be like the Most High.

Well, simply because he saw how glorious it was. So he actually saw the glory of God and, instead of the fear God, he chose to reject the fear of God. It is a choice.

See another account here in Ezekiel 28:11 – 19

Verse 14. "You were the anointed cherub who covers;
I established you;
You were on the holy mountain of God;
You walked back and forth in the midst of fiery stones."

Being an anointed cherub who covers means:
Exodus 25:20 – 22, Numbers 7:89, Psalms 80:1, Isaiah 37:16

So, as these readings reveal, Lucifer was an anointed cherub who covers and saw the glory of God, but decided to choose otherwise and not choose the fear of God.

Another example is found in Genesis 2 and 3. Adam and Eve saw God, and had daily encounters with Him, they saw His glory. Yet, they ignored the fear of God and chose otherwise. It was their choice.

See what Romans 1:18 – 19 says:
All these people made the choice not to fear God even when all that needs to be revealed about God and His glory had being made known to them. They saw all that needed to be seen, yet they chose not to glorify Him as God or fear Him. They all decided never to choose the fear of God.

Job 21:7 – 15.
Verse 15. "Who is the Almighty that we should fear Him? And what profit do we have if we pray to Him?"

A person may see all there is to be seen and choose never to fear God, while another may not even see anything, or probably see just a little and choose the fear of God.

The fear of the LORD is more so a decision of the heart and will.
Daniel 1:8, 3:1 – 18.
Apart from the fear of God that is born out of an encounter with God, far stronger and more effective, is

that which is born out of a solid decision to fear the LORD always.

The reason for this is because as mortals we tend to forget and also easily lose the intensity of awareness given to us through experiences as time and age goes by.

I was made to understand some years ago that man's ability to forget is one of those healing mechanisms God puts in us. Of a truth without our ability to forget, some wounds (hurts) will never heal because the memory of them makes the wound fresh again.

Also, this forgetting ability we all have in us wears out the intensity of the consciousness we carry after an experience that was desirous or un-desirous. Our choices are often born out of the intensity of such consciousness, only a few have theirs born out of the decisions they made. These are the matured ones. They are not moved by experiences but by decisions. This category of person's fear of God comes through decisions rather than just experiences.

Imagine the three Hebrew boys. The realities of the moment was the world ruler (Nebuchadnezer)
threatening them, the blazing fire in front of them, and all the armies of Babylon against them.

It took more than just a revelation or an experience of many years ago to have given them the impetus to decide who to fear at this point. It was a decision.

Daniel 3:18. "But if not, let it be known to you, O king, that we do not serve your gods, nor will we worship the gold image which you have set up."

How was it that Lucifer rejected the fear of God. Simply because he never made it as a choice, talk more of as a decision. Besides, as we found out earlier, our fear of the LORD stays our focus on Him making our trust or faith in Him to remain rigid. To stay that focus on God takes decision.

Analyze this in light of king Nebuchadnezer.
He saw and heard Daniel reveal the dream and its interpretation. A dream no one knew. And Daniel told him God Almighty did it.
He was also given the chance to see the supernatural deliverance of Hananiah, Mishael, and Azariah from the blazing furnace. Yet Nebuchadnezer only celebrated God briefly as the consciousness of the experiences remained fresh. As soon as this intensity waned he

forgets God. He never did fear God until Daniel 4:28 – 37. Here he finally made the decision to fear God after God taught him a bitter lesson.

"The fear of God that will keep a man going is that which is born out of decision not mere experiences because experiences fade with time."

Even the love that survives is that which comes through decision not mere heart beats.

Recall this truth from Pastor E. A. Adeboye again to heart **"The fear of the Lord is the climax of spiritual maturity."**

Putting all of these together in light of the explanation that unified faith and the fear of God, we can say therefore that:

"After a revelation of the glory of God or before it, our decision to fear God instills the fear of God in us, and this becomes a driving force for our faith."

And faith itself never says No. It does not back out or back down.

Qualities Of The Fear Of God

What qualities can one see or observe in the sun? Some include: Light, heat, and energy to mention but a few.

What qualities then marks out the fear of God?

One can better answer such a question by examining the qualities of God because this fear drives an individual to behave and react based on God's character.

1. Love is a quality most undeniable. This encompasses all the other qualities that will and can be mentioned. I Corinthians 13:1 – 13.

2. Forgiveness. The life of Joseph perfectly depicts this quality of the fear of God. Genesis 50:15 – 21. The fear of God propelled Joseph to forgive easily. Despising the fear of God will undermine and erode the virtue of forgiveness which is a panacea to bitterness and vengeance.

3. Selflessness. According to Exodus 22:25 – 27, this command by God can only be kept by anyone who fears God, not minding how much he/she lent.

4. Faith. Without much talk on this quality since it has already been treated, it is worthy of note to reveal Exodus 14:31.
   Also Exodus 9:20 – 21. Those Egyptians who began to fear God took steps of faith as it relates to the word that God gave Moses for the land and the soon to come supernatural occurrences. Yet some did not give any

regard to God and took no steps of faith to save their servants and their livestock.

5. Contentment. Exodus 18:21. "...hating covetousness..." These men feared God and hated covetousness. The fear of God is what makes a man desist from desiring what belongs to another man. Things like another person's wife, husband, properties etc.

6. Humility. Conduct a Study of all the characters in the bible that had the fear of God, one thing that is easily noticed in them is humility. This, in itself, is an attribute of God.

7. Prosperity. Acts 9:31. The fear of God in the churches brought the needed multiplication and increase. That is what we need in the church today as we evangelize. We must mature in our fear of God. The fear of God offers us all the increase the church of Jesus Christ in our generation longs for and even more. Genesis 22:12 – 18.

Unprecedented increase came to Abraham when his actions showed that he feared God.

8. Listing all these without mentioning wisdom will definitely be incomplete. Hear Job 28:28. "And to man He said, 'Behold, the fear of the Lord, that is wisdom, And to depart from evil is understanding.'"

Besides, several verses in scripture points this truth to us: Proverbs 9:10, Proverbs 15:33 and Psalm 111:10. Wisdom is a great quality to have when one has the fear of God.

See what God says concerning the fear of God: Genesis 22:18
"In your seed all the nations of the earth shall be blessed, because you have obeyed My voice."
What was God implying?

Genesis 22:12. Paraphrased:
"Through your action Abraham, I now see that you fear God, since you did what I said you should do."
Verse 18. "...because you have obeyed My voice."

From God's explanation here, to fear the LORD is prompt and total adherence to God's command. Total and prompt obedience.
This calls for wisdom, the kind of wisdom for searching the scriptures through the help of the Holy Spirit in order to know what God is saying and then obeying it.

Finally: Psalm 25:12 – 14 says
"Who is the man that fears the LORD?
Him shall He teach in the way He chooses."

168

"He himself shall dwell in prosperity, And his descendants shall inherit the earth."
"The secret of the LORD is with those who fear Him, And He will show them His covenant."

God will choose the right way for the person who fears Him and teach him about the way chosen for him to walk.

The fellow shall not only prosper, but shall peacefully relax in his prosperity with non to scare him away. Example is Abraham.

And because this fellow feared the LORD, even his descendants became big beneficiaries. They are to inherit the earth. Note that it is not merely a village or city, it is the earth that they shall inherit. "The earth" means the earth.

In closing, the things that only God knows are with those who fear the LORD. That fellow is made to know secrets.

God will show them His covenants. That is a very high level of secret. Covenants are high level secrets. So God is saying: "If you fear me, even the deepest secret of all secrets will be shown to you."

May God strengthen us all to make decisions to fear Him daily in Jesus name.

PRAY

- Heavenly father, enough of childish play, instill Your fear in me in Jesus name.
- Heavenly father, it is time to fear You daily, strengthen my will to fear you promptly and totally. Isaiah 11:3
- I decree, the fear of God in me will not fade or die in Jesus name. It shall wax stronger in Jesus name.
- (call your name thrice), you will live and move in the fear of God always in Jesus name.
- Isaiah 11:2. Father, fill me with the spirit of the fear of the LORD in Jesus name

APPENDIX

Some things to stay away from in order to live a daily victorious life above fear.

- All forms of satanic movies:
  Horror movies
  Magic / witchcraft movies
  Pornography
  And all other kinds.
  Beware of cartoons with subtle messages carrying demonic undertones.
- Ungodly songs and rhythms. You should know that songs are a form of worship. Most of these circular musicians worship devils and are into occultism. When you sing their songs dedicated to devils you are actually inviting those devils.
- Ungodly and satanic designs on wears, paintings, art work.

And other things the Holy Spirit points your attention to.

HELPFUL BIBLE PASSAGES AGAINST FEAR.

- Romans 8:1 – 4. Condemnation inspires fear, so this verse can help you to deal with fear, caused by condemnation.
- Ephesians 3:12 and Hebrews 4:16. When fear of not accessing God's favor and presence sets in.
- Psalm 46:1 – 5. When everything seems overwhelming and seems to totally consume us.
- Psalm 18:3 – 6 and James 5:14 – 16. When sickness or disease seems to overwhelm us. Also I Peter 2:23 – 24.
- Psalm 18:3 – 6. When satanic arrows of ungodliness buffets the mind and fear of falling into sin sets in. Also Jude verse 24. Follow through with discipline.
- John 14:1 – 2, Philippians 4:19, Psalm 23:1 – 3. When material, financial and such kind of lack seem to break us down.
- Psalm 127:3 – 5 and Isaiah 8:18. When confronted with the fear of negative attitudes of children, or of children going wayward.
- Psalm 79:11, Psalm 118:17, Psalm 91:16. When the fears of death confronts us.
- Psalm 121:1 – 2. When the fear of having no helper tries to overwhelm. Also Psalm 72:12.

- Isaiah 54:14 – 15. When confronted with the hordes of shame and disgrace.
- Isaiah 41: 10 – 13. Against the fear of worries. Any worries.
- Isaiah 35:4, Psalm 34:4. Standing against fears.

PRAYER FOR EVERY READER

Heavenly Father, we all have lost sense of Your fear, please forgive us in Jesus name. Have mercy on us all

- Heavenly Father, I pray for every member of the body of Christ worldwide, bring us all back to the consciousness of Your fear in Jesus name.
- Heavenly Father, as You gave Jesus Christ the Spirit of the fear of the LORD, pour out this same Spirit on the body of Christ worldwide in Jesus name.
- Heavenly Father, we ask, let the fear of the LORD be the driving force and the reason behind our actions from today in Jesus name.
- We open ourselves up O God for the workings and dynamics of the fear of the LORD in our lives in Jesus name.

www.ingramcontent.com/pod-product-compliance
Lightning Source LLC
Chambersburg PA
CBHW022008090426
42741CB00007B/946